TEN OF THE BEST

Memories of Ten Independent Schools in the New Elizabethan Age

Latymer Upper School
Frays College
Leighton Park School
St Lawrence College
Harrow School
Welbeck College
Whitgift School
Dean Close School
Highgate School
Magdalen College School

Richard Martin

Oxford 2021

Author's Note

I would like to express my thanks to Oliver Godfrey for drawing the illustration on the cover especially for this book and to those who have encouraged me to record my scholastic adventures, especially Brian Joplin, Curtis Rogers, Father Robert Sweeney, my former Vicar, and Anne Dutton for her eagle eye in correcting my typescript.

ISBN No: 9798515615765

Preface

As I approach my eightieth birthday, I feel it is time to set down some of my memories of over forty years of schoolmastering before they become too dim to recall. I never planned to make teaching my career, but Fate seems to have taken me by the hand and led me through a wonderfully varied succession of independent schools. Already, when I look at particulars of the schools today, with a plethora of Deputy Heads, pastoral and ancillary staff and, in many cases, co-education I realize how much the schools have changed. Recent lurid revelations in the press about the pressures current sexual mores are putting pupils under, naming some of the schools included here, have made me wonder what has gone wrong. I fear the blame must lie primarily with our society today, which the schools simply reflect.

I have wished to be as honest as possible in my recollections of schools and colleagues and I would like to stress that the schools I describe are very different places today - for better or worse. I am deeply grateful for all the happy memories they have left me with. If I have given offence or upset any former colleagues or pupils in what I have written, I can only ask for their forgiveness. As has been written elsewhere recently, in a different context, "Some recollections may differ."

Note

I have included each school's motto in the relevant chapter heading. For those with no motto I have included an appropriate, if slightly irreverent, phrase. For Welbeck College I have used the Portland motto.

The Author outside the Common Room, Magdalen College School, Oxford.

Chapter One

Paulatim Ergo Certe

Latymer Upper School, Hammersmith

In early September 1952 I pushed open one of the tall double doors that opened off the vestibule outside Latymer's School Shop. I was an eleven year old boy waiting with Mother to be fitted out with my school uniform. I was spellbound by the sight that met me: a towering Gothic hall, lined with tall Gothic-shaped boards on which were inscribed the Oxbridge scholarships and Higher Level Distinctions won by previous pupils. My name was to be added seven years later and is still there. Below the boards, against a background of shiny brown encaustic tiles, were hung two rows of portraits of Headmasters and other worthies. Above them were Gothic beams and windows. Down the centre of the Hall, receding into the distance, where I could make out a gallery with an organ to one side, was a line of black iron chandeliers.

My awe-struck gaze was called back to life with the sharp words, "Next please," as I let the door swing back and was led into the very congested storeroom that served as the school shop. I was soon fitted out by Mr Armstrong (who, I later discovered, also taught Maths) with the regulation black blazer, with the school crest embroidered on the breast pocket, cap with the crest again, and two pairs of shorts- one black for football and one white, for gym. Then came the football shirt, stockings and gym vest. Finally, I was presented with a Bible (Authorised version- I still have it), a Pocket Oxford Dictionary (which I also still have, sitting on my desk as I write), a geometry set in a sliding-top box and a hymn book (both long abandoned).

The Great Hall, Latymer Upper School

Such was my introduction to the school where I was to spend most of the next eight years as an 11plus Middlesex Scholar. I had previously visited the school for a morning to take its entrance exam, but I can only recall that it involved some complicated code one had to decipher. I felt I had failed miserably, so it was quite a surprise to find myself being offered a place in Form 2G with our form-master Mr Grauberg, himself an Old Latymerian (one of half a dozen in the Common Room) and a Modern Linguist. We were taught Mathematics by Mr Whelan, a benevolent elderly Welshman of whom I still think when I hear his favourite Welsh hymn 'All Through the Night. ' It used to be popular at funerals. Mr Whelan was teaching us one Autumn day in 1952 when news came of the terrible three train railway crash at Harrow and Wealdstone Station. I remember his concern that boys like me, living in that part of Middlesex, might have difficulty in getting home by train after school.

Our Headmaster, Freddie Wilkinson, was a man who put boys first. He had a great rapport with us and his morning assemblies in the Hall often overran, to the masters' annoyance! He could be very emotional, as on the occasion when Soviet tanks came on to the streets of Budapest at the time of the Hungarian rising against Soviet domination. I shall never forget his breaking down in front of the whole school. It is still etched in my memory.

One of Freddie Wilkinson's frequent themes at his assemblies was that his generation had made a mess of the World. It was up to us to do better. To that end, he was instrumental in setting up links with the Johanneum School in Hamburg in 1947. The first exchange visit had taken place in July 1948 with a visit from Hamburg. The next summer Latymer boys visited the city that British bombs had flattened just a few years prior. The link has endured ever since. The school also set up an International Society, under the auspices of the Council for Education in World Citizenship, and a branch of the Royal Commonwealth Society. In the Sixth Form, parties of boys visited the Society's headquarters (outside which the words 'Royal Empire Society,' carved deep into the stonework, had been ineffectively altered to 'Royal Commonwealth Society.') I remember particularly the jamboree that marked the Gold Coast's transition to Ghana and the hopeful aspirations that were soon to be dashed by Dr Nkrumah's autocratic rule. It was not as easy as had been assumed for Westminster style democracy to make the transition to tribal Africa. It was to be demonstrated time and again during Britain's retreat from Empire.

The school roll at Latymer had reached the 1,000 mark by my second year, Wilkie having announced we now numbered 999 boys plus one mouse! We were tightly packed standing throughout the Assembly in the main Hall, but we knelt for prayers on the hard floor. Towards the end of my time it was suggested that this was a dangerous practice in such crowded conditions, but the boys obstinately continued to kneel - except for the prefects, of which I was by then a member, and the masters, who stood against the walls.

Wilkie had brought the school through the Second World War, when it was evacuated to Slough. He loved to stroll around the school and talk to boys informally. He was the inspiration behind the annual summer MAD (Musical and Dramatic) Evenings for which the Hammersmith Town Hall's auditorium was hired. He even composed a tongue-in-cheek school song ('Latymer's the Place for Education') in the absence of an official one. These events were great fun. I remember a particular trio of boys in the year or two above mine who played a group of eccentric old men, including a vicar (that boy, after serving in the Royal Navy, became a much loved priest in the East End of London and then at King's Lynn) and a querulous musician (who became a distinguished music critic)

Prayers: Latymer 1950s

The MAD evenings were a by-product of the school's strong dramatic tradition. The Gild, a dramatic society for sixth-formers, had been founded back in the 1920s, with later junior branches- the Apprentices and the Journeymen- for junior and middle school boys. In the 1950s the dominant characters were the Reve, our Head of English, Wilf Sharp, the Publick Oratour, George 'Bert' Offiler, Head of History, and our Head of Classics, Geoff Grimsey. These three men made a tremendous contribution to the life of the School and influenced generations of boys for the good.

In addition to the MAD evenings, at the end of the Summer Term, the Gild held its Jantaculum at the end of the Autumn Term. The casts for the various dramatic sketches and musical items were a mixture of masters and boys. One of the most popular acts, which featured for a number of years, was the Festival Trio, comprising of Wilf Sharp, as the bluff, very English bass, the Assistant Latin master Mr Lineham (a vicious beater) as a greasy Italianate tenor and Geoff Grimsey as a very aged all-rounder. They always brought the House down!

When the time came for Wilkie to retire his was a very hard act to follow. His replacement was Kenneth Sutcliffe, a rather dour Northerner and a devout Methodist, to whose orange juice a large tot of vodka had been secretly added at the annual Oxford Old Latymerians' dinner, when he attended as our guest. It had no effect at all! A few years ago I was amused to hear Sir Ian McKellen, the very 'out' actor, say that Kenneth Sutcliffe was his uncle! It seemed quite inappropriate. Whereas Wilkie was a charismatic personality who roamed around the school talking to his charges, Ken, a shy man, was study-bound and buttoned-up. After he had been Headmaster for a term or so there was a rather embarrassing outbreak of graffiti around the school proclaiming, 'Ken must go,' which the Second Master, 'Archie' Davies, had to speak about to the school, without actually mentioning the offending words, of course.

Things settled down in due course and Mr Sutcliffe showed himself to be a very decent, if uncharismatic, Headmaster with high standards and great integrity. When a friend of mine went to tell him that he had been awarded an Open Scholarship at St John's College, Oxford he was met with the 'encouraging' Headmagisterial response, "Are you quite sure?" My own leaving report contained the prediction that, "At this rate he won't get into any university, let alone Oxford or Cambridge." When my mother met him later, by chance in Oxford, Sutcliffe had the good grace to inform her that he had been wrong about me three times. After I completed my Oxford degree at St John's, I had hoped to spend the practical term of my Diploma in Education course at Latymer, but was refused. Several years later, when teaching down at Ramsgate and wishing to be nearer home, to help my mother look after my father, who had developed early Alzheimers, I applied for a teaching post at Latymer and was again turned down.

Since the school gym had been destroyed by a bomb in the war, for most of my time at Latymer gym was taken in the school hall, that imposing Gothic space that had so impressed me on my second visit to the school. Since it was surrounded by classrooms that opened directly off it, the location was far from ideal. In class we became inured to the sturdy gym master's cries of, "Up, up, up," as his charges ran on the spot, or pounded around the hall! Where we changed, I cannot remember, but I'm pretty sure there were NO showers! I was amazed to find a similar lack of facilities nearly 50 years later at my last teaching post at Magdalen College School, Oxford, where boys were accustomed to change before and after games in their house rooms, which doubled as teaching rooms. They preferred to avoid the official changing rooms since bullies were prone to stuff their kit down the lavatories there! Now girls have been admitted to the Sixth Form, this practice has no doubt been curtailed!

Latymer's main Games field was located at Wood Lane, close to Wormwood Scrubs prison, around which we were sometimes sent on runs in inclement weather. Some of us, however, would divert into the Savoy Cinema at East Acton, if a boy could be persuaded to pay an entrance so he could open the side door to admit the rest of us, for a much needed warm-up. The wonderful thing about Latymer in those days was that there was only one Games afternoon a week, because of the limitations of Wood Lane, and there was little attempt to teach us how to play. Those who wished to abstain, after changing into games kit, were mostly left alone to indulge in deep conversation on the edge of the soccer pitch, hoping to avoid the ball. Later on I got out of soccer altogether by pretending to play tennis, before I switched to swimming at the old-fashioned municipal Lime Grove baths where we all picked up verrucas!

The walk from Latymer, via Shepherd's Bush, to the Lime Grove baths was through quite a rough area, now gentrified and highly sought-after by television types from the BBC at White City! There were two impressive Anglo-Catholic churches which in later years attracted me. Sadly the big-boned brick Butterfield church of St. John the Evangelist in Glenthorne Road is now part of Latymer's sister girls' school, Godolphin and Latymer. But Brooks' Holy Innocents still thrives.

Back in the 1950s, school building projects were rare. Apart from the rebuilding of the gym (in its turn, now long superseded) I can only recall the dramatic driving of the Cromwell Road extension across the middle of the school playground. The compensation paid for the school to acquire houses in the adjoining road which have now been pulled down to make way for new school buildings. Access to the 'river' side of the school, after the road came, was provided by an underpass through which we used to pass daily for lunch in the school canteen, an unprepossessing prefabricated structure, which, unfortunately, matched the food that was served there. I soon opted out, to eat sandwiches provided by my long-suffering mother in my form room, or later in one of the little hideaways one found around school, such as the top floor in Rivercourt House or the Quiet Room next to the Chapel, at the top of a tall building on the corner of King Street, which housed the Geography and History Departments at that time.

The Chapel had been Latymer's last clerical Headmaster, Dr Dale's, final legacy to the school in 1937. It was dedicated to the Chantry Schoolmasters of England, as a fine inscription on the door proclaimed. The Revd 'Monty' Cann had been School Chaplain since 1935 and remained until 1958. He was what was known as a 'Modernist' in his religious views, but was also a firm disciplinarian. Woe betide the boy who came bottom in his frequent Divinity tests, when 'Slammy Sammy,' a table tennis bat on which he chalked a multi-coloured target, and 'Excalibur'- the cane - were flourished before being applied to the unfortunate boy's posterior! First the target, then the cane. In spite of what would now be regarded as beyond the pale, he was a popular figure and he made sure he taught all the junior forms for Divinity once a week, so he and they could get to know each other. Wilkie took the Sixth Form Divinity in his study. Holy Communion was celebrated before school on Wednesday mornings in the Chantry Chapel. When I became a school Chaplain nearly forty years later I followed a similar pattern, without the corporal punishment, of course!

Back in the Fifties corporal punishment was quite usual, and there were some savage beaters amongst the Latymer staff, although Freddie Wilkinson much preferred a solemn talk with miscreants, which was usually far more effective! Monty suffered from painful gout attacks, when he would limp down the corridor with one foot bound up, leaning heavily on his stick. He died in office while I was in the Sixth Form. Until a new Chaplain, the Rev. John Evans - hence 'RevEv' - could take up his post, my friend Michael James and I as, respectively, Head Server and Chairman of the Christian Fellowship, had a fairly free rein in the chapel. We used to delight in reciting very 'extreme' litanies during the lunch-time Intercessions service, mainly to annoy a Chemistry master, who was also a Baptist minister, whom we suspected of having designs upon the Christian Fellowship.

Most boys joined Latymer aged 11, in the Second Form, since the First Form was part of the small Preparatory Department, based on the ground floor of Rivercourt House, a lovely large Georgian house on Upper Mall, which faced the River Thames. Rivercourt also accommodated the Sixth Form Library, a peaceful oasis on the first floor with lovely views down river towards Hammersmith Bridge and up river towards Chiswick Eyot. I was to spend happy hours there dreaming of owning such a house. Use of the graceful curving main staircase was forbidden, since it was said to be fragile and unsafe for use by boys. So we used the back stairs, which gave access to other rooms, in poor repair, such as the room where we had French conversation with Madame Cooper in the Sixth Form. There were gashes in the plastered canvas that formed the inner wall covering, revealing London brickwork. Further upstairs was a room which housed the Gild wardrobe. This was an unofficial cosy retreat for some of the more artistically-inclined Sixth Formers.

By contrast, the Prefects' Room was a crowded room off the main corridor close to the inside washroom and urinals. The outside cubicles are best unmentioned. The Prefects' Room was the scene of frantic perusal of the Bible each morning by the prefect due to read at Assembly, since in my day there was no pattern of readings laid down by the Chaplain.

Latymer's delightfully relaxed attitude extended to the school's Combined Cadet Force, which was entirely voluntary. I was thus able to avoid it without having to undertake some unpleasant alternative activity, which was how some schools kept up numbers in their nominally 'voluntary' CCFs, as I was to find out later in my teaching career. I was dragooned into serving as an Officer in the Army and then the Navy sections of three different school corps! Only ordination eventually freed me from this irksome obligation.

During my time in the Fifties at Latymer, the CCF was in decline. It was still presided over by Major 'Tom' Stewart, an OL who had suffered serious injuries during the war. He had a trick of being able to pass water from his mouth to exit from one ear, to our impressed amazement. He taught

Maths in the Middle school with heavy reliance on corporal punishment. By the time my younger brother came to Latymer, in my last year, Major Stewart was getting a bit past it, and, in particular, the CCF was run in a very slapdash fashion, leaving boys like my brother, who had joined it on my advice as a good way to become a Prefect, free to nick various items, including actual guns! To this day he is fond of party tricks like exploding cakes!

By the time I reached the Sixth Form at Latymer, compulsory games were so nominal that I was able easily to dodge them in order to take the short journey on the District Line to join my father for lunch at his office in the Middlesex Guildhall, now the Supreme Court, in Westminster. Afterwards I sometimes drifted into the salerooms behind the Army and Navy stores or Harrods' salerooms, then at Trevor Square in Knightsbridge, just across from the famous store. I am writing now at the desk I bought then for £7!

Another freedom I enjoyed when I reached the Third Year Sixth, with a very light timetable, centred on Oxbridge Scholarship preparation, was to come and go as opportunity offered through an easily opened window in one of the houses the school had acquired in Rivercourt Road, adjoining the school. The house had been pressed into service as the English Department, prior to its demolition to make way for a new teaching block.

In those distant days Oxford and Cambridge colleges were organised into three or four groups for the purposes of joint entrance or scholarship examinations. These started in the Autumn Term after one had taken A Levels the preceding summer. In 1959 Merton College Oxford held an entrance exam in November, before the main groups. Unusually, one sat this college's exam at school. It was arranged for me to take it in the Second Master's study, completely unsupervised. I still recall struggling with temptation to consult his large dictionaries during the French and Latin translation papers for the History Entrance Exam! Perhaps that distraction helped to ensure my failure. Then it was off to Clare College, Cambridge in early December for their Scholarship Exam. I was accommodated in their impressive 'New' Buildings by Giles Gilbert Scott, across the Backs and the River Cam from the old college buildings. I was interviewed by their eminent History don, Professor G. R. Elton, whose "England Under the Tudors" was a standard textbook at that time. But it resulted in another failure. Next, in January, came the Entrance Exam at Brasenose College, Oxford where I had a room high up in the front quad just across the passage which separated the college from St Mary's, the University Church. The chimes of the church clock gave me disturbed nights and again I wasn't offered a place. By then the fees charged by colleges to take their exams and the charges for travel and board were beginning to mount up, but there were three more shots in my barrel! First came St Catherine's College, Cambridge which had close connections with Latymer, with a distinguished OL, Canon Waddams, as a Fellow. But, again, there was nothing doing.

My penultimate shot was the Scholarship exam at St. John's, Oxford. Following perusal of the 'Oxford University Gazette,' as we were encouraged to do individually at Latymer, I had already established contact with the college by writing a letter of application for a place to the President, Dr Costin. I had received a courteous and welcoming reply, explaining that all candidates were asked to sit the Scholarship Examination, on the results of which places would also be offered. The group of Oxford colleges to which St John's belonged occupied the last of three possible slots that year, by rotation. So off I went again, in early March 1960, to stay in St John's and sit the examination, which was held in the dauntingly large dining hall of nearby Keble College. One was beginning to get to know the faces of some of the candidates by then - but each time there would be a lucky group missing, who had already obtained their places (unless they had just given up trying!) At my interview with the two distinguished St John's History dons, Howard Colvin and Keith Thomas, I recall being asked if the college was my first choice. I dissembled, admitting to having tried 'some' earlier colleges 'for practice.' Mercifully they didn't press the point and I was able to mention my earlier letter of application to the President. When I came to be interviewed by him and a full panel of Fellows, and was asked why I had applied to St John's, I was able truthfully to say that, as a High Anglican, I was attracted by the college's association with King Charles I, whose Archbishop of Canterbury, William Laud, had been President of St John's. What I didn't know was that Dr Costin had recently published a study of William Laud! So I was putting my head into the lion's jaw! Fortunately, the benevolent President let me, as a callow youth, off lightly and I was to my great relief awarded a place at St John's for Michaelmas Term 1960!

That left me free for the Summer Term. I would no longer have to face the 'last chance saloon' - St Catherine's, Oxford and Selwyn College, Cambridge. These two colleges held their exams as late as May. It was cynically suggested that, as relatively recent and poorer foundations, they kept themselves afloat financially by all the fees they garnered in from the desperate remnant remaining unplaced!

So, how to spend that glorious free summer term? I had not yet caught the travel bug, and anyway, back in 1960, options were still very limited. So I fell upon an advertisement in our local paper for a master to teach English and General Subjects at Frays College, Uxbridge!

Chapter Two

Facilities for Hot Lunches

Frays College, Uxbridge

I was still only 18 years old when I took up my Summer Term teaching post at Frays College, Uxbridge. Faced with a free summer term after leaving school, before taking up my place at St John's College, Oxford in October 1960, I had noticed an advertisement in the local paper for a Teacher of English and General Subjects to O Level. Well, I had been a School Prefect, so why not give this a go?

Frays College was one of a number of small independent day schools in that part of North West Middlesex that catered mostly for pupils who had failed the 11 plus examination for entry to a Grammar School and whose parents didn't want them to go to the local Secondary Modern School and could afford to pay the modest fees at such a private school. The school was situated a little way out of Uxbridge on Harefield Road, but it had previously occupied other premises. Eric Blair, alias George Orwell, taught French there for a term in 1933, before contracting pneumonia. Like me, he possessed no previous teaching experience - but he had been a King's Scholar at Eton! By 1960 there were just over 200 pupils from 5 to 16 and a staff of 12. I succeeded the Vicar of All Saints, Hillingdon as a form master and teacher of English, with French - which Orwell had also taught! My French was not up to much, in spite of Mme Cooper's conversational efforts in the Sixth Form at Latymer, and I concentrated on translation from French into English, as a safer bet than English into French! Apparently, these days standards have slipped so much that it is all that is generally now required for O Level French.

Frays College's blazers and matching caps were a wonder to behold. Broad stripes of maroon and blue were separated by a vivid apricot coloured stripe. They certainly made the point that this was a PRIVATE school!

There was nothing fancy about the school's buildings in Harefield Road, which backed on to the River Frays, a tributary of the River Colne, which eventually ran down to the Thames. They consisted of a large Victorian house, to which had been attached a very basic three storey building in plain brick. The Headmaster taught in what had been the main ground floor reception room of the old house. It was also the Fifth (top) form room. His study was across the passage adjoining the new addition. He and his wife, who I believe cooked, or at any rate supervised, the school lunch each day, lived upstairs in the house.

Lunch was an important feature of the school- it figured prominently in the weekly advertisement for the school carried in the local papers: "Frays College, Uxbridge. Education for Girls and Boys 4-16. Facilities for Hot Lunches. Headmaster H.S.K. Stapley, B.Sc.(Lond.)" Mr Stapley only died in 2020, aged 93. I remember him as a bluff, no-nonsense Northerner. He was of medium stature, but carried an air of authority, notably when he took morning Assembly in the large room which served as the school hall. As an 18 year old, I would have said he was in late middle age, but he can have only been in his thirties at that time.

The monthly pay cheques were signed for 'Kent Lodge Ltd,' as proprietors of the school. I understood they were a group of local tradesmen, but have no further information. As for the lunches, they were good, as far as school meals go. We all sat down at two or three long tables, according to seniority. The food was served to us at the tables. A favourite dish was the meat pie that appeared regularly until a food inspection, after which it was withdrawn and replaced by a slice or two of cold spam with pickles! Apparently the pie had involved the reheating of meat already cooked, which was condemned as unsafe. But it was delicious! Fish and chips were always served on Fridays.

As advertised, the school was coeducational, which was a new experience for me. I was given no lessons on keeping order, other than to keep classes occupied and mark their preps punctually. Corporal punishment had been the long stop at my own school and I am ashamed to admit I had to resort on occasion to the slipper, or even the ruler, for younger pupils, as administered to me at my kindergarten. One very difficult boy refused to be slippered in front of the class, so I marched him down to the Head's study and waited outside to make sure he got his desserts there. Which he did.

One afternoon a week was set aside for Games. There was a Games and PT master on the staff, but occasionally I was called on to help with cricket matches. There was no games field attached to the school, so we had to walk up to a pitch on the common for matches. So much for my summer term at Frays. I little thought I would be returning there after I had taken my degree, or, indeed, that I would make teaching my career.

It was only after a boring job with Osram (GEC) as a trainee Organisation and Methods Officer, after finishing college, that I was to return to Frays in October 1963, having noticed an advertisement in the local paper for my old job, "with immediate effect." I broke the news that I wanted to leave to my senior colleague at Osram, who was taken aback, but agreed that, if I was really sure industry was not for me, there was no point in my staying to serve out my notice. So I was able to return to teaching just over three years after going up to university. I had kept in touch with Frays during my student years as they had kindly invited me back for the staff Christmas lunch each year. It was a completely different atmosphere from my experience of industry- warm and humane.

When I returned to the chalkface, I found little had changed at Frays. Sadly, a favourite colleague, a lady who had taught History, had died in the ladies' lavatory at the school, thus causing the immediate vacancy. So this time I was able to teach some History, instead of the dreaded French, as well as English. It went well and I found I was enjoying life a great deal more than I had at Osram. There was also the prospect of generous paid school holidays, which I must confess were certainly a compelling reason for changing from Osram with just two or three weeks holiday a year. Like many others- John Betjeman and Evelyn Waugh come to mind- I found the prospect of being chained to a desk for most of the year, after the freedom of Oxford, to be almost insupportable. Teaching offered me a way out, as it has to many of my friends. 'Those who can't, teach,' as the old jibe goes, is a cruel saying. I would say, rather, that those who put an absorbing life and the privilege of working with the young above financial reward have made the right choice. Certainly, I never regretted my own choice, even at my lowest moments.

Having decided that my future lay in a teaching career, I needed to take steps to lay a proper foundation. This meant applying for a Postgraduate Certificate in Education year at some university. I hoped to do this at Cambridge, and thus be able to see more of the friend I had made when, at the invitation of our Latymer History master 'Bert,' I had joined a group of sixth-formers from the school on an expedition to investigate Roman roads up in North Wales. We had kept in touch since then and he was now in his first year at Trinity Hall, Cambridge. Alas, I was informed by Sir Fulque Agnew, the impressively named Director of the Cambridge Department of Education, that my Oxford Third Class Degree in Modern History was not a sufficient entry qualification for the Cambridge course. In desperation I tried Homerton College, then the teachers' training college on the edge of Cambridge, but was informed only women were admitted there! So I finally settled on the London University course based at Goldsmiths' College, New Cross.

The next step was to apply for a temporary post in a recognized Headmasters' Conference school, which could offer me some experience of Sixth Form teaching, as well as the junior classes. I noticed an advertisement in the *Times Educational Supplement* for a temporary English Master for two terms at Leighton Park, a Quaker boys' boarding school on the edge of Reading, which I was duly offered after an interview with the impressive Old Wykehamist Headmaster, John Ounsted. He asked me how I maintained class discipline and I confessed to occasionally resorting to corporal punishment at Frays. "Well, you won't be able to use that here!" I was informed in no uncertain terms. As a Quaker foundation, Leighton Park followed pacifist principles long before corporal punishment was abolished in state and independent schools. One of the things for which I am deeply grateful to

Leighton Park was that it stopped me from becoming a beater, like several of my masters at Latymer. I learnt to use my powerful voice to drown any backchat in class. Hardly ideal, but it worked! Then there was the matter of my degree- an Oxford Third in Modern History. It didn't seem to worry the Headmaster in the least! He took the line that any English gentleman who was reasonably well read could teach his own language and its literature. I found out subsequently in my long teaching career that, while some Headmasters had Firsts, at least as many had Thirds like me. And, as for teaching English- well, those with a degree in the subject were often in the minority!

It was difficult breaking the news of my appointment at Leighton Park to Frays College, since I had grown fond of it and had enjoyed joining their Christmas Common Room lunches while I was up at Oxford. I felt I was letting them down. But experience in an HMC school would stand me in much better stead when the time came to apply to such schools for permanent posts. And I had, at least, been able to cover an awkward gap for Frays' in their often rather make-do staffing arrangements.

Chapter Three

Quaker Oats

Leighton Park School, Reading

So the Spring Term 1964 found me taking up my post at Leighton Park. I was given a study in Reckitt House, one of the four senior boarding houses that accommodated the 275 or so boy boarders between the ages of 13 and 18, and the furthest from the main school buildings. It was a ten minute walk or so across the large park in which the school buildings were situated to the main building with its plain, but elegant Quaker meeting hall, Masters' Common Room and teaching rooms. I was given a pleasant form room of my own, which is always an enormous help. However, there seemed to be a shortage of suitable plays to read in class in the book store and I remember borrowing a set of Terence Rattigan's 'The Deep Blue Sea' from the public library to read in school!

The avuncular Second Master (who had a portrait of Oliver Cromwell in his classroom) took me under his wing and told me that, if I had any difficulties with the Headmaster, I should feel I could confide in him to sort matters out! This used to be the way when Second Masters were usually appointed internally, on the basis of seniority. From around the 1990s that all changed. Second Masters were renamed Deputy Heads and were generally appointed from outside. They were usually ambitious young men anxious to please their Heads, who would then support their applications for Headships, after they had made a name for themselves shaking up the Common Room and generally upsetting things for a few years! Certainly they could no longer be relied upon as a nervous young teacher's friend in need! To my mind, it's been one of the most significant changes in the whole ethos of the public schools and one certainly not for the better! Others might disagree if they see schools in terms of management. Indeed, Heads of Departments are now sometimes referred to as 'line managers' without any apparent irony!

Every Thursday morning the first lesson was taken up with a traditional Quaker meeting in the main hall. The benches were arranged facing each other across a central aisle. There was no hierarchical order of seating- masters were mixed up with the boys and there was no formal order of service or hymn-singing. Everyone was free to stand and speak when moved to do so 'in the Spirit of the Meeting,' irrespective of age. To my polite surprise, it worked very well! We sat in silence until someone was 'moved by the Spirit.' Serious and less serious contributions were made from time to time by both masters and boys. I was even moved to speak once myself!

On other mornings there was the usual kind of morning assembly in the hall, called 'Collect,' with the masters ranged behind the Headmaster on the stage. On Sunday evenings there was a straightforward service with hymns (from 'Songs of Praise') readings, prayers and an address, sometimes by a visitor, and not always a Quaker. On Sunday mornings one was free to do as one liked and I was given the Head's permission to take a small group of boys who were so inclined downtown to the Anglo-Catholic parish church of St Giles. The headmaster explained to me that he had High Church sympathies himself! And my Housemaster also told me he had grown up in a Birmingham Anglo-Catholic parish and he found some similarity between the silent Quaker worship and the old silent Mass. He was now a Quaker elder down at the Meeting House in Reading, as were a number of other masters.

On Sundays, when I was not taking boys to church, I would enjoy a drink or two after Mass on my way back to school. On return to Reckitt House I would be confronted by one of three large joints of meat at the end of each long dining table for the 60 or so boys in the house. It was wise not to have imbibed too much as one set about carving for the hungry boys! One of the disadvantages of presiding at the end of the table would be that boys would be asking for seconds as one tried to get through one's own last-served meal. Not good for one's digestion! Apart from House lunch each day I was invited by the Housemaster, Len Stables, and his wife to share their meals in their private dining room. I also had my bedroom and bathroom on their side of the house.

Quaker connections were still strong at Leighton Park. There was a Cadbury on the Board of Governors, harking back to the days when Britain's chocolate industry was controlled by the three Quaker families of Cadbury, Fry and Rowntree. The future Labour leader Michael Foot was an old boy and other members of the Foot family were prominent in the school's recent history. David Lean, the distinguished film director, was another old boy.

The Spring and Summer terms whisked by in this delightful setting. Easter came early in 1964 and the School Term continued until the following week. This was not unusual in boarding schools at the time, but what *was* unusual was that teaching continued throughout Good Friday as a normal school day. I discovered that Quakerism didn't have any sort of liturgical calendar. Later on I heard that a colleague of mine from my next school, St Lawrence College, who was a very keen officer in the School's Combined Cadet Force, had moved on to Leighton Park and had actually attempted to set up a branch of the Cadets there! This was a step too far for the pacifist Quakers! He moved on after that.

Leighton Park School: View of Peckover Hall in Autumn

I made a number of friends amongst the senior boys and masters and their wives and still have a striking outline portrait of the head of one of my sixth formers, executed by one of his school contemporaries and presented to me as a leaving present. Both my teaching and house duties went well and it was intimated to me that I could stay on the teaching staff permanently if I gave up my place at Goldsmiths' College to read for the London Postgraduate Certificate in Education, popularly known as the 'Dip.Ed.' While required for teaching in Local Authority Maintained schools, this qualification was not obligatory in an independent school. I was severely tempted, but I was advised by the Department of Education that the Certificate might well become a requirement in all schools in the not too distant future. It never has! But I was also tempted by the idea of an extra year of student life! So I politely refused the offer to stay on at Leighton Park and stuck to my commitment at Goldsmiths' College.

The college was located at New Cross in South-East London, a two hour journey by tube from my parents' home in Pinner. Consequently I had arranged accommodation in one of the Halls of Residence a short distance from the College. This proved to be very different from College life at Oxford. We had to provide name-tagged napkins, towels and bed linen. A rising bell rang at about eight each morning. I found I had very little in common with most of the residents, who were four years younger than me and often studying technical subjects or Art, Goldsmiths' having an unusual role as an independent college as well as being a constituent of London University, for whose Certificate I was a candidate, rather than the alternative course and certificate offered by Goldsmiths. This meant all my lectures were on Friday mornings in Senate House in Bloomsbury, halfway to home. My tutorials in Goldsmiths were few and far between and my teaching practice in the Spring Term 1965 was to be at Harrow County Boys' Grammar School, convenient for my home in Pinner. After a week in residence in Raymont Hall I decided it would be more pleasant and economical to commute from Pinner. I still have some tagged napkins as a reminder of my brief residence in Raymont Hall.

Since Mondays to Thursdays at Goldsmiths were free, I obtained a job teaching in an old-established, but long disappeared, London tutorial college, or 'crammer,' called McNalty and Burrows in Pimlico. I learnt a good deal more of practical use in my subsequent teaching career there than I did at Goldsmiths' and I got paid into the bargain! The establishment was housed in a grand terraced house in St George's Square. Teaching took place either in the basement or the attic. The large rooms on the intervening floors were occupied by the aged Principal, Mr McNalty. Burrows I think was long dead. What was striking was that the walls of the private rooms were covered with beautiful Pre-Raphaelite pictures, which must have been worth a fortune. The Principal had been up at Oxford around the same time as Evelyn Waugh and he proudly showed me original copies of the *Oxford Broom* magazine, which Waugh had edited.

The actual teaching at McNalty and Burrows was not demanding. Groups were small - half a dozen or so - for both O Level and A Level English. The pupils were pleasant, but not very bright, girls and boys who had nearly all been at independent schools, where they had failed the relevant GCE examination, or needed a better A Level grade to gain admission to the university of their choice. The establishment kept large numbers of past papers and working through these formed the basis of one's teaching. Not very imaginative, but it was what the customers wanted and it brought the desired exam results! A careful analysis of past papers, and the frequency with which various topics came up, proved rewarding in deciding on which topics to concentrate. I found this approach paid dividends when I was landed with 'O' level re-take classes at my first 'proper' teaching post! And I'm afraid that it has become increasingly the case that parents see the high fees they pay independent schools primarily as a way to ensure good exam results. And the schools, with some notable exceptions, have pandered to this by taking part in 'League Tables' of examination results. So much for the broader education they prided themselves upon! In saner times such tables were regarded as the province of crammers, not of proper schools.

Chapter Four

In Bono Vince

St Lawrence College, Ramsgate

During my 'practice' term as a student teacher at Harrow County Boys' Grammar School in Spring Term 1965, where I reckon I must have taught Michael Portillo History (all those Bradshaw's!), I started applying for my first permanent teaching post. It proved to be trickier than I had anticipated.
I visited the Oxford University Appointments Committee's offices and discussed matters with Mr Dunsmore, who looked after posts in schools. Although I had read Modern History at St John's College Oxford, my temporary post teaching English to A Level at Leighton Park had convinced me that my path lay in that direction. The Department of Education at London University had insisted I teach History, since my degree was in that subject, during my practice term at Harrow County Boys' Grammar School. I found it irksome being tied closely to a syllabus, whereas teaching English one was much freer to roam as one fancied and teach what one liked. So I was applying for English to A Level posts on the basis of my Third in Modern History.

I also wanted to be resident in a boys' boarding school, since I had never been forced to look after myself since leaving home and had vowed never to be in the position of some of the younger bachelors on the staff of Harrow County, who were to be seen shopping in the supermarket after school for something to eat, back in their miserable lodgings. So Mr Dunsmore put me on his list for English posts in boys' boarding schools and I started applying with my 'full Curriculum Vitae and two testimonials, together with names of referees' as advised.

I also took the precaution of visiting the well-known private school agency Gabbitas-Thring in Sackville Street, off Piccadilly, London W1. Those who have read Evelyn Waugh's hilarious novel *Decline and Fall,* based on his own experiences as a prep school master on coming down from Oxford, will doubtless recall Paul Pennyfeather's visit to Mr Levy at Church and Gargoyle, Scholastic Agents. Having read it, I was well prepared for my visit to Gabbitas-Thring, whose old fashioned offices bore a distinct resemblance to their literary counterpart's. Many of the schools for which Gabbitas acted were listed as 'Private,' rather than 'Public' schools. In other words, they were not members of the Headmasters' Conference, to which all the top schools belonged. Many of them were still run as private profit-making companies, like Dr Fagan's establishment Llanabba Castle in N. Wales, in Waugh's novel, or Frays College, whereas the HMC schools had to be non-profit making charities. I tried to steer clear of the former and concentrated my efforts on vacancies notified in HMC schools. But often I would receive notices for the same HMC posts from both Gabbitas and Mr Dunsmore.

As the Spring Term wore on I began to get some interviews and eventually I was faced with a choice between Worksop College, Nottinghamshire and St Lawrence College, Ramsgate. For Worksop I was interviewed by the Headmaster, Roger Northcote-Green, in the old Public Schools Club in Piccadilly. I was reassured to find he had the same degree as I did, but his games qualifications were much more impressive than my almost non-existent ones! What attracted me to his school was that it was an Anglo-

Catholic foundation, part of the Midland Division of the Woodard Schools. I noted from the prospectus that it had an imposing chapel, with six impressive candlesticks gracing the altar. I later learnt that these were on loan from the Duke of Newcastle and some years later they were returned to the family for the altar in the Duke's private chapel at Clumber Park. Worksop was a long way North and remote, in that part of Nottinghamshire known as the Dukeries, because of the number of stately ducal homes in the area.

St Lawrence College

St Lawrence, by contrast, was easily accessible by the Southern Electric railway. The line actually ran through the school grounds and the compensation paid by the railway company had provided the finance for the impressive Chapel. But, inside, the Chapel was very austere, in contrast to Worksop's. Plain glass in the windows (since replaced by a modern John Piper/Patrick Reyntiens East window) and no candles at all on the altar! Just two brass flower vases in their place. St Lawrence was firmly Evangelical, having been founded by the South-Eastern Clerical and Lay Alliance as a counterblast to the Woodard schools. As an Anglo-Catholic this naturally worried me, but my visit to the school put my fears at rest. I was frank in my interview with the Headmaster, the Revd Canon Ronald Perfect, about my own religious affiliation and he assured me in his avuncular way that, if I respected the College's religious tradition, they would respect mine. (I had confessed during the interview to worshipping in Pusey House, a very 'High Church' institution, at Oxford!)

Chapel at St Lawrence took the form of a compulsory short morning service every morning, with a hymn, which was practiced on Saturday mornings. On Sunday there was a voluntary early service of Holy Communion, followed later by a service for the Junior School. The Senior School attended Choral Evensong on Sunday evenings. Copies of *The Public Schools' Hymnal* were neatly placed along the shelves in front of each boy's place. Term began traditionally with the hymn, 'Lord behold us with Thy blessing, once again assembled here' and ended with 'Lord dismiss us with Thy blessing.' Unlike many schools, the chapel was conveniently joined to the main school building by a passage through Courtenay House's territory. Underneath the Chapel was the College's spacious Library. Because the Chapel was joined to the main school building it was also used as the Assembly Point for the termly fire practices, until it was pointed out that it would be extremely dangerous in a real fire for us all to be crammed into a building with only one narrow passage for access, plus a basement door leading up to the Vestry. But one advantage of the narrow entrance at the West End of the

Chapel was that each boy had to pass under the gaze of the Headmaster, installed in his pew there and well placed to check if a boy had polished his shoes.

Outside the well-stocked Library was a cabinet displaying the engine nameplate from the St Lawrence steam locomotive that had, up until the 1950s, each term pulled the School Train from Charing Cross down to Ramsgate. The Southern Railway had a whole series of these impressive locomotives, each named after a different Public School in its region.

Canon Perfect was nearing the end of a long teaching career spent entirely at St Lawrence. The son of missionary parents, he had been a boarder at the College in the 1930s before going up to Cambridge to read Theology. He was a Hockey Blue and International as well. Returning to his old school, he had soon been put in charge of the Junior School, which was a Preparatory School in its own right and on the same site. When war broke out he moved to take on the Headship of the Senior School, which was evacuated from its prominent site above the English Channel to Courteenhall in Northamptonshire.

After the war Perfect had supervised the College's return to war-ravaged Ramsgate. Fortunately the College buildings had not been hit, but conditions were fairly primitive. One of the three long-serving bachelor housemasters told me when I joined the staff that he would never have come, had he seen Ramsgate, or the College, but he had been interviewed by the Headmaster in a Midlands railway waiting room! I was interviewed in the Headmaster's office, which was strategically situated just inside the main gate of the school. I learnt when I joined the College that, since suffering health problems, the

Headmaster moved from his office down to his house after lunch. He could often be seen exercising his dog in the school grounds from midday onwards, his black Homburg hat well pushed back on his head. In the afternoon, he would be up on the Games field or showing prospective parents around.

St Lawrence attracted me, situated as it was within easy reach of the sea. Its position at the back of the town, close to the railway station, was not as appealing as the dramatic picture conveyed in the prospectus, which managed to suggest, without actually putting the claim into words, that the college had a dominating position overlooking the English Channel!

I liked the young Head of English and several of the other masters that I met on my interview day. So, when the offer of a resident post to teach English to A Level came – and I still hadn't heard further from Worksop - I was glad to accept it.

Unfortunately, I had received notification of the vacancy at St Lawrence from Gabbitas-Thring's agency, as well as from the OU Appointments Committee, so I duly received a demand for Gabbitas' commission fee when they received news from the school of my appointment. Since I had already thanked Mr Dunsmore at the Appointments Committee for his help in securing the post, I was not disposed to pay Gabbitas commission. I told them that I had taken up the post with the Appointments Committee's assistance, but they persisted. Eventually the matter came down to whose envelope containing the job details I had opened first. Naturally, I was able to assure them that I *always* opened the Appointments Committee's missives first.

Later on I received a welcoming letter from Jim Sandison, the Housemaster of Manor House, inviting me to become his House Tutor. There were five boys' boarding houses at that time, plus a day boys' house called Newlands and a new venture: Cameron House, for boys from 11-13. This was a far-sighted initiative of Canon Perfect's to tap into a new market, as distinct from the feed from the Junior School. The Junior School had a very good reputation as one of the leading prep schools in the very crowded prep school population of Thanet, but not all the boys came on to St. Lawrence. There were at least five prep schools still operating in the area in those days, a relic of Victorian convictions of the benefits of sea air and a bracing climate. Up on the St Lawrence playing fields one was acutely aware that there was little between them and the Urals on the other side of Europe!

The Headmaster extracted two promises from me during my interview. Firstly, I had to promise not to marry for three years, since he was dependent on resident bachelors to supervise the five boarding houses! Next, Perfect had noted from my Curriculum Vitae that I had been a member of the Oxford University Officers' Cadet Corps. Would I agree to take a commission in the school's Corps? Of course, I agreed to both conditions. Serving as an Officer in the CCF with my almost total lack of military experience proved to be a chore each week. I had not been in the voluntary CCF at my own school and had only joined the Oxford OTC to gain access to its very pleasant Officers' mess. My military activity at Oxford was limited to turning up once a year to qualify for membership by 'firing my musket!' Perhaps because of this, I was put in charge of the Artillery section of the CCF at St Lawrence. Once a term there would be a Field Day - an expedition to a military establishment or perhaps an exercise in the Kentish countryside. This was all fairly undemanding, under the benevolent gaze of the CCF Commanding Officer, who taught Science.

St Lawrence College CCF Inspection Day Parade
(Author in centre)

The Artillery Section possessed a huge Bofors Gun which could be revolved on its turntable and manoeuvred up and down. If the College really had been situated up on the cliffs dominating the English Channel it would have been very impressive indeed! We had dummy ammunition cartridges to load but, unfortunately, one of these jammed during my second year or so and after that I spent the subsequent Annual Inspections dreading discovery! Fortunately, it went undetected. My little group in the Artillery section were understanding chaps who helped me cover up our deficiencies, but there were some very keen cadets in other sections who were focused on an army career. The Senior Under Officer, or senior boy in the CCF, was fearsomely smart on parade. He retired as Head of the Army General Staff some years ago and for a time after that was Constable of the Tower of London! I still read his trenchant views in the press from time to time.

My accommodation was not immediately to be in the College itself, but in Sutton House, a 'Waiting House' a short walk from the college gates. This was a base for about a dozen boys awaiting vacancies in their chosen senior houses. The house was presided over by the genial Head of Science, Mr Dixon and his charming wife Kate, who also acted as a relief Matron in the school's Sanatorium. The new Cameron House was accommodated in the former San, the days of large-scale school epidemics mercifully being over. In Sutton House I was given a bedsitting room, next to the house bathroom, which boasted two baths! I was nonplussed when Kate Dixon breezily asked if I would mind if she popped into the other bath while I was there! Of course, she was just teasing a callow young master - but I was always a bit nervous on bath nights! The boys used the same room earlier in the evening, of course. There was also a rather repellent latrine, fortunately separate from the bathroom.

Each morning of my first year I made my way through the College gates and up the drive to the impressive red-brick turreted College building, which accommodated the five boarding houses, Chapel and Dining Room, as well as the Masters' Dining Room (Matrons dined separately) and Common Room, in what had originally been the Headmasters' quarters. A pleasant separate house had been built in the college grounds for the Headmaster in the Nineteen Fifties, together with houses along College Road, towards the Station, for the Chaplain and the two married housemasters. Their two houses had bachelor tutors resident in the main block, since there was no accommodation for married housemasters. As I trudged up the drive towards the looming building (christened 'Colditz' by some of the boys) I confess I looked forward to the time I would be able to move on to a more congenial school. Of course, when the time came to leave at the end of my fourth year, it was all I could do not to burst into tears, as I remembered retiring masters used to do sometimes at my own school!

Manor House was accommodated on the first floor of the building. I was promised a study in the main block and, after my first term, I was found a room up on the third floor, between two dormitories belonging to Grange House, which was split between the ground and third floors, and opposite the Grange House bathroom and lavatories. It was not the most peaceful of retreats while the boys were bathing and going to bed! The Tutor's bedroom and bathroom (with no lavatory!) for Manor House was still occupied by the bachelor who had been Tutor until he had been appointed Housemaster of the 11plus Cameron House. Since he was still being paid the Manor House Tutor's allowance I was asked if I would mind foregoing an allowance since I was clearly well off! The evidence of my wealth was my new Triumph Vitesse Sports Coupe, but I had to point out that, far from demonstrating my wealth, it demonstrated my need of income to pay the hire purchase! So I was eventually granted the small tutor's allowance. Free Board and Lodging was also included, so it was not a bad deal.

As Christmas approached at the end of my first year, I was interested to see a notice about the 'Staff Entertainment' appear on the Common Room noticeboard and innocently enquired what form this would take. Would there be a Common Room Glee Club, perhaps? Or would we play Charades? I was soon disabused of any such ideas. "Oh, no, the Staff Entertainment is for the STAFF," I was informed. The penny dropped: the "Staff" meant the College's domestic and secretarial staff, not members of Common Room, in other words, the teachers. It's a nice old-fashioned distinction that has now almost disappeared. Having been taught it, I tried to keep to it as long as I could when editing school magazines, for example. What now usually appears, I fear, under the graceless heading 'Staff List' was headed instead, 'The Common Room' and masters were listed below, for many years in order of seniority. I fear that the disappearance of this distinction has been accompanied by a change in the attitude of many headmasters towards the Common Room. Canon Perfect always used to knock on the door and ask permission to enter our Common Room, even though it had originally been the Headmaster's Drawing Room before a new house had been built for him. I've heard of other heads who followed the same polite custom, but all that has gone, and I'm afraid teachers (not 'masters' now!) are so often regarded by the new breed of Head as 'staff' to be hired and fired as required.

After my first year, the previous House Tutor, whose family, incidentally, was said to own the Eaden Lilley Department store in Cambridge, moved out to Cameron House and I was allocated his small bedroom, adjoining its own bathroom but with no lavatory. Next door was a very noxious boys' lavatory and one urinal. This was quite inadequate for 60 boys, so it was reserved for prefects and the rest of the house had to go down to the ground floor 'Cloisters.' Showers were further, down in the basement where the games changing 'alleys' for all five houses were located. I got into the habit of going downstairs each evening to use the Bursary's commodious lavatory.

The boys' spartan dormitories were located off a central passage. Each dorm had a row of washbasins, with cold water only, at one end of the room. There was a jug for hot water, which had to be fetched from a tap located by the latrine. Now I read in the current school prospectus that pupils have ensuite facilities in their own rooms! Curtains, run up by the College Caterer, only appeared in the dormitories towards the end of my time. Each boy's bed had a shelf over it with an army ammunition box on it, in which smelly socks could be placed and sealed. There were hooks for clothes, but no wardrobes. Matron supervised the issue of clean linen, underwear, socks and shirts each week. And, judging by the laundry book I found, my predecessor was equally economical with his changes of clothes!

Further along the passage from my bedroom, in the opposite direction from the dormitories, was the Second Master's bedroom and opposite was his bathroom and a study for the non-resident married Housemaster, who came in for a certain number of days during the week. But weekends were mostly the house tutor's responsibility. At the end of this passage, through a pair of doors, was the newly relocated San, on what had been the Headmaster's bedroom floor, above the Masters' Common Room.

The Second Master, another bachelor known to colleagues as Drage, was a formidable figure. He would stand in the quad outside the entrance to the teaching block at the beginning of school and after break to catch any boys- or masters- who were late for class, shifting his weight ominously from one foot to the other as he examined his watch. His study was next to the Masters' Common Room, just by the Masters' Entrance. He had been Head of Classics and was a lover of Wagner. On evenings when things hadn't gone well he would retreat to his study and play his Wagner records at top volume. Then one knew to tread carefully! Underneath the imposing exterior he was friendly to callow young masters and eventually I was invited out to dine with him at his favourite Burlington Hotel, down in Folkestone. The deal was that I did the driving, but we got on very well. I was extremely sorry when he died in harness towards the end of what would have been his final year. It couldn't have been more dramatic, since he collapsed at Top Table in the Dining Hall during lunch. The Headmaster was sitting next to him and it wasn't clear for a while which man had been struck down, as they both slid under the table. The school had to file out respectfully, leaving behind the jam roly poly puddings.

Another less upsetting dramatic incident occurred on another occasion during lunch in the Masters' Dining Room, when supplies of tinned tomatoes ran out and a colleague took it on himself to visit the Lady Caterer in her office to enquire if there might be some more. He was refused; but, showing initiative, he marched into the Dining Hall, past the serried ranks of boys, up to the Top Table, which had its own oven to keep food and plates warm. And –lo and behold!- sitting inside was a spare dish of the sought-after tinned tomatoes! But at that moment the Lady Caterer, Miss Fisher entered the hall! So our brave colleague was caught red-handed! Not to be intimidated, he boldly confronted her with the enquiry, "Well, what do you call these?" She peremptorily ordered him to leave the dish alone. So Derek just dropped it in front of her, leaving her in her bespattered white overall, while he marched out of the hall! In the Masters' Dining Room we remained blissfully unaware of this battle being fought on our behalf until an enraged Lady Caterer appeared in the said overall! Two of my more misogynistically-inclined colleagues used habitually to cover their heads with their napkins should any female intrude into our sanctuary, but on this occasion a number of us were forced to resort to such methods in order to conceal our mirth. I was told later that the Headmaster, whom the Caterer supplied with various goodies down at his house, had actually threatened to horsewhip the miscreant master when she reported the matter to him!

In the evening at dinner the resident bachelors were served a three-course meal in the Masters' Dining Room at 7pm, the boys having to make do with a more spartan supper in the Dining Hall at 6pm. This was served with piles of bread for them to fill up any gaps, together with slightly strange tasting tea from a large urn. I was solemnly informed by a senior boy that the tea was dosed with bromide to calm down any erotic urges the boys might have at night! I thought it best not to pursue that matter. But I did, however, feel it incumbent upon me to pursue a related matter. Tuesdays, Thursdays and Saturdays were half days, with the afternoon and evening free for games and activities. Town leave had to be obtained from the duty master in each house, and was strictly controlled. I used to take advantage of being free from teaching and off duty in the House on Thursday afternoons by either driving over to Canterbury to hear Choral Evensong in the Cathedral and indulge in Afternoon Tea in the Cathedral Tea Rooms by the gate to the Close, or taking the train up to London to see a show or meet with friends. The last train back to Ramsgate left London Victoria at 11. 10 pm, and arrived at Ramsgate around 1.10am. It was just a ten minute walk down from the station, along College Road and into the main building. I used to walk from one end of the House to the other along the passage between the dormitories. One evening as I passed I became aware of a disturbance coming from one of the dormitories. I opened the door and put on the lights to find all the beds had been pushed aside, leaving a large central area covered with mattresses from the beds. Evidently I had interrupted some kind of dormitory feast, or perhaps worse. Each dormitory had two senior boys as prefects, but this method of control was obviously dependent on the character- and inclinations- of the prefects in charge. The boys scampered back to their beds after restoring their mattresses and pulling the beds back into line and I said no more. However, I felt I had to mention the incident to the Housemaster when he came in the next day. He in turn reported it to the Headmaster, who- as reported back to me- merely observed that it was simply 'animalism!' The two prefects were given a stiff telling-off and the matter was sensibly dropped. I know not whether the alleged dose of bromide in the tea urn was subsequently increased.

The Second Master's demise meant that I inherited his bedroom as a study, and also his bathroom opposite, which had the luxury of its own lavatory. However, I discovered I was expected to share this with visiting referees on games afternoons! The room next door, opposite the Housemaster's study, had been converted into a Sixth Form dormitory, with a row of basins with hot and cold water taps. It always amused me, while I was sitting in my study, to hear the Headmaster conducting prospective parents on a tour and claiming this as a '*typical* dormitory!' I was tempted to call out, 'Ask to see the others!' but, of course, I refrained, mindful of my job!

Along with the Second Master's former bedroom and bathroom, I also shared his steward, or scout, who cleaned a number of the masters' rooms and even polished our shoes, if I recall aright. Dennis - for that was his name - was a slightly simple chap, as were a number of the College servants. It was rumoured that the Bursar had an arrangement with some local institution for such people. I'm ashamed to recall that the traditional boys' slang used to refer to the domestic staff as 'the apes.' Dennis also served us bachelors at dinner, except on Sunday nights, when there was a cold buffet after Evensong and married colleagues were known to slip in for a knob of cheese, provided the Lady Caterer was not in sight. One evening, as he leaned over the table serving the soup, I noticed Dennis was wearing one of my ties! I kept quiet, but checked my wardrobe after dinner and found the blue patterned silk tie from Liberty and Co was, indeed, missing, as was another yellow and red foulard silk tie. So I bided my time and - sure enough - on a later evening Dennis was sporting that one! I plucked up my courage and asked Dennis where he had got the tie. "Marks and Spencer, Sir," was his po-faced reply. I was particularly annoyed by this, since they were Liberty ties and greatly superior to M & S's products. Nevertheless, I contained my indignation and consulted the Bursar the next day. "Well, the only thing to do is to have Dennis in my office in front of you and put the question to him again," the Bursar decided. I just couldn't face possibly getting poor Dennis the sack, so I said we'd better let the matter drop. At least my pointed questioning of Dennis at the table had the desired effect and no more ties went missing!

Another resident bachelor who died in harness during term was the Director of Music, Dennis Cocks. He lived in an eyrie at the very top of the five-storey main building, to which few were invited. I was not one of them. He used to dine on what I thought of as the Silent Table in the Masters' Dining Room, in company with the Housemaster of Courtenay and the Maths master with the wandering hands, who eventually moved on to a prep school. There was a fourth place for anyone who did not relish talking during their meal. Usually there were two other tables regularly set for dinner: the one presided over by the Second Master with the other two Evangelical bachelor housemasters on either side of him and, again, a spare seat at the end. The third table was much more of a free-for-all, where my friend Patrick, the Head of History, was often found with a couple of younger colleagues. Obviously, one tried to join them if the fourth place was still free and one wanted some conversation. From time to time there was discussion over whether the Matrons and Caterer might be invited to dine with us, but this was strongly opposed by the traditionalists, on the grounds that the ladies would want to talk about boys' ailments during dinner, it being assumed that they would have no other topics of conversation.

The Director of Music was unusual, in that he never played the organ in Chapel and was never seen at worship either. One wondered if he had some conscientious objection to Christianity; but, if that was the case, his seemed an odd appointment at a school like St Lawrence. There were rumours that he had had a row with the Headmaster many years ago and had been forbidden to enter the Chapel as a consequence. He had a pleasant young assistant, Fred, who played the organ and generally assisted with the music. After the Director's sudden death it was assumed that Fred would take over his duties, but it was not to be- an outsider was appointed. Fred was then told that his own post would cease to exist and he must look elsewhere. Imagine his surprise and embarrassment, therefore, when he was shown an advertisement for his post in *The Times Educational Supplement* by the Headmaster of another school during his interview there!

The nearest theatre to St Lawrence was the Marlowe in Canterbury and I was soon organizing regular outings for groups of boys to suitable plays. On one memorable occasion our coach, chartered from the local bus company, came to a standstill in the middle of the country. I dreaded an explosion from the driver about some boy's misbehaviour that I had not noticed, but - to my relief - the reason turned out to be that the coach in front of us had broken down and he had stopped to offer assistance. It didn't take long for a row of adolescent Lolitas' faces to appear in the rear window of the bus in front, gesticulating in what was meant to be a seductive manner. This had a dramatic effect on the boys in our bus who rose to the challenge by making what I can only describe as a baying noise, like animals on heat. Fortunately no intercourse between the two parties was possible, marooned as they were in their separate coaches! My memories of this incident have been triggered by the current explosion of newspaper stories about sexual misbehaviour by boys in co-educational public schools, in which my old school, Latymer Upper, figures prominently. There were very good reasons for keeping teenage girls and boys in separate schools! At Latymer the authorities also made sure that we were let out of school at least half an hour after our sister school, Godolphin and Latymer. Godolphin School in Hammersmith had been a boys' school that was rescued by the Latymer Foundation in the early years of the twentieth century, on condition that it became a girls' school. Unfortunately, when Latymer lost the Government Assisted Places Scheme and found itself having to take "too many Indian boys" as it was put to me by a senior master, they decided to renege on the former agreement with Godolphin and take girls as well. Now they are wringing their hands about what cynics would say was the inevitable result, sad comment though it may be on adolescent urges, now inflamed by unlimited access to online pornography.

There was a deeply embarrassing occasion when I found myself called up before the Headmaster to explain why I had read a poem to my class which contained THE four letter word. This had come about after I had an altercation with a boy who persistently defied me by closing a window that I had ordered him to leave open. I had punished him for disobedience. At our next lesson he produced a poem which he said he had enjoyed: could I read it out in the lesson? I glanced at it and it appeared to be worth reading. However, as I turned the page, the dreaded word appeared a few lines ahead. What to do? Chicken out and skip it? I decided to be bold and press on with reading out the whole verse. The miscreant, disappointed no doubt by my sangfroid, had reported the incident to his parents, who had promptly telephoned the Head to protest at my 'choice' of 'poetry!' I explained how it come about to the Head and received a stern warning not to repeat such a poem. He might have added, "And to prepare your lessons properly," but he was too realistic for that.

One term there were also coach expeditions from St Lawrence to Earl's Court in London to attend Billy Graham rallies, in which I did not partake. No doubt this was a sincere effort to convert wayward youths, but it smacked to me of undue emotional pressure and I doubt if its lasting effects, if any, were beneficial. I write as one who himself attended a Billy Graham film in his youth, which was followed up afterwards with the usual invitation to go forward and receive counselling. The Baptist gentleman to whom I was assigned put me in touch with our local vicar who, as a good Anglo-Catholic, came round to see my parents and ask them what they thought they were doing in permitting me to attend such an event! I hadn't even told my parents about it!

Ramsgate is one of three resort towns on the Isle of Thanet. I had previously stayed at Margate with my parents at the end of the war. By the mid Nineteen Sixties it was still rather rundown, its chief asset being the enormous Dreamland Amusement park. Nowadays it has undergone a renaissance with a branch of the Tate gallery on the sea front and its connection with the artist Tracey Emin.

Broadstairs was much more salubrious, with its quaint centre and narrow street running down to the Tartar Frigate pub and the harbour, where Edward Heath, the Prime Minister, who grew up in Broadstairs and attended the local Grammar School, kept his yacht, as did the larger-than-life Housemaster of Tower House at the College. Broadstairs has a pleasant sheltered beach, overlooked by the Royal Albion Hotel. Next to that used to be Marchesi's Restaurant, an Italian-owned family restaurant which was a great favourite of several members of the Common Room at St Lawrence. There was also an Italian Ice Cream Parlour, one of a local chain named Morelli. I taught one of their sons in the Fifth Form at St Lawrence.

Winters could be harsh down in Thanet in the mid 1960s. One usually got through the Michaelmas Term to Christmas without too many problems, but driving back to school along the Thanet Way in January could be taxing. One always knew when one was back on the Isle of Thanet (not really an island - it was only cut off by a small stream) by the stench of rotting cabbages and, especially, Brussels sprouts! They were cultivated in huge fields across the island! As one passed Manston aerodrome, much used in WW2, the smell was unmistakable! Welcome to Thanet!

From my second year on, an advantage of being accommodated in the same block in which the House was situated, along with the Masters' Dining Room, Common Room and Chapel, was that one didn't have to brave the winter weather at all. The teaching block - a fairly new addition, but built in a last gasp of Gothic style - had been connected by an arch to the main building. An unfortunate result of this enclosed life during the winter months was that, for the only time in my life, I found I was suffering from constipation. Eventually this necessitated a rather humiliating visit to the School Doctor, which culminated in an undignified procedure.

There were, of course, occasions when one would have to turn up on the games pitches, above the railway line, to support house or school matches, but I didn't have to wear Games kit as I had got myself put in charge of swimming, down in the old-fashioned school pool, between the College buildings and the Junior School. The pool's chlorination was somewhat haphazard and I never ventured into the water myself. We swam against a number of nearby public schools and it was interesting to compare their facilities on away match fixtures. The Duke of York's Royal Military School at Dover had the best pool, but they were mostly a rough crowd. The furthest fixture was against Westminster School, which in those days used the pool underneath the flats at Dolphin Square. A number of our boys had failed the Common Entrance examination for Westminster and had come to St Lawrence as their second choice, so this fixture could be a bitter-sweet occasion for some. But at least St Lawrence did have its own pool, now long replaced by a modern one, of course.

After we had marked the Common Entrance papers each year and adjusted our pass mark to accommodate virtually all the candidates, we would have a Common Room meeting with the Headmaster, who would report on the next year's potential numbers. They were usually short and he would announce with a sigh, "Well, I suppose I'll have to dredge the pool." Somehow or other numbers crept up, whether from the mysterious 'pool' or elsewhere, until the College was financially viable for another year. But one could certainly see why the 11plus house had been started to provide an additional intake! The Common Entrance Exam was taken by most prep school pupils, but the pass mark was flexible! It was left up to each school to decide its own pass mark. And there was no official mark scheme provided, so schools could easily adjust their results to avoid the shame of being seen to take applicants with very low scores. At my next post, at Harrow School, we took it in turns to mark the English CE papers. When it was my turn, I remember being told by the Head Master to bump up the English marks, so our intake looked more discriminating than we could afford it to be!

Because of the precarious finances of St Lawrence in those days there were some nervous moments. I remember particularly when the late arrival of our salaries into our bank accounts one month caused panic amongst masters with mortgages and other outgoings to meet. On another occasion, the Bursar managed to hit the front page of *The Daily Telegraph* by dramatically lowering the fees slightly for the coming year. He explained that finances had turned out better than had been expected when the fees had been fixed the previous year; but, of course, it looked as if it was a desperate bid to gain additional pupils! On another occasion the same Bursar circularized masters with details of a private pension scheme which he suggested would be more beneficial than the Government scheme to which, by then, nearly all Headmasters' Conference schools belonged. My Head of Department was very quick to counter this with a circular explaining the advantages of remaining in the Government scheme- chiefly that its benefits were inflation-linked and guaranteed by HM Government. This affair left a nasty smell, since it was obvious that *someone* would be getting lucrative commission for each master who transferred to the private scheme. The Bursar retired soon afterwards. His wife was much missed by some of the more adventurous younger masters, with whom she had been particularly friendly!

During my fourth year on the staff (1968-9) girls were admitted to the Sixth Form, initially as day pupils. St Lawrence was quite a pioneer in this, following the example of Marlborough College and a few other HMC schools. It came about when the local private girls' school, St Stephen's College in Broadstairs, got into financial difficulties, after the Headmistress eloped with her female Secretary. So St Lawrence took in the remnant of St Stephen's Sixth Form. Two pleasant girls joined my English set. I well remember my Head of Department enquiring after I had left and he had taken over my set, teaching 'Hamlet,' how it was that only the boys had notes explaining some of Shakespeare's bawdier references. I explained that I dealt with such passages when the girls were absent. It would have been very embarrassing to explain such matters to them in mixed company and one could be fairly sure the examiners would not set questions on such passages! I well remember reading 'Hamlet' in the

Lower Sixth at my own school with the Chaplain, who also taught English. Our texts were ancient bowdlerized editions and 'Monty' Cann, the Chaplain, insisted on reading out and explaining the censored passages! So I was well prepared!

Towards the end of my fourth year, and the first year of girls in the Sixth Form, Canon Perfect raised the subject of how the girls had settled in. "Well, I think it's all gone very smoothly," he observed. I couldn't resist undermining his complacency a little by observing rather tartly (remember, I had already got my next job lined up!) "Well, if you overlook the couple I found writhing together on the floor under one of the Library tables, I suppose it has." Reading all the brouhaha in the press and on television at the time of writing, about girls being sexually harassed or even raped in what are mostly former boys' schools, reminded me of this incident at St Lawrence. As far as I know there were no further such incidents reported. It's noticeable, in fact, that the schools like St Lawrence and Dean Close in Cheltenham that have been fully co-educational now for some fifty years have not been named in the revelations on line and in the press. I would suggest that it may well be because they have been properly run as Christian co-educational establishments for a long time, rather than having recently taken in a limited number of girls to bolster Sixth Form numbers!

It was notable how times (or finances) had changed when girls were admitted to St Lawrence just a year after boys had been banned from visiting St Stephen's, following a joint school dance, supervised by both Heads sitting on a dais overlooking the dance floor! This, in itself, was a daring innovation. I had previously been amazed to see pairs of boys solemnly waltzing round a room, under the supervision of our visiting lady dance teacher! This lady, whose son was a day boy at the school, was also a tower of strength in rehearsing any dances that might be required in my Head of Department's all-male Shakespearean productions. Even after girls were admitted to the College, it took a while for them to be allowed to take female roles in the annual Shakespeare play, since – after all - the parts had originally been written for boys! The Shakespeare play was always performed at the end of the Spring, or Lent Term and the first performance was a matinee to which local prep schools would be invited. The Head of English was a gifted producer and the standard was extremely high for a smallish school. Productions were even sometimes reviewed in *The Times.* I acted as Stage Manager and Props Manager and this took up a lot of one's spare time towards the end of the Lent Term, when one was usually suffering the after effects of flu by then! I still have memories of stifling my bouts of coughing in the wings off stage!

Towards the end of my time *King Lear* was given, with an exceptional boy in the title role, who went on to act at Cambridge. The producer insisted that real sheeps' eyes should be used in the terrible scene where Gloucester is blinded. When Edmund gouged his eyes out – "Out, vile jelly!'- he flung the sheep"s eyes, previously concealed in his hands, down on to the stage. Those in the front seats practically vomited! I hate to think of the lasting effect it may have had on the prep schools who were invited to the matinee!

The next year *Measure for Measure* was chosen, and the Headmaster was apprehensive of its sexually explicit theme of corruption and hypocrisy. It was only allowed to go ahead when appropriate scriptural references were added to the posters and to the programme, to make it clear that the Bard was on the side of the angels, in his attack on false puritans.

I produced Arnold Wesker's 'Chips with Everything,' one term, with a view to bringing the school drama a little more up to date. I had also produced it at Leighton Park, where its anti-establishment theme went down rather better with the Quaker foundation than it did with the Evangelicals and the school Corps! The play is set mostly in an RAF station and has an almost entirely male cast which made it a good choice, although at Leighton Park, with no CCF, I had to borrow RAF uniforms from a local Catholic school! When I asked my boss at St Lawrence why he always produced a Shakespeare play as the main offering in the Lent Term, he explained that, with all the disruption a School Play causes, there was a great deal to be said for staging a really worthwhile play, with a large cast to provide the boys with many opportunities for acting. And I think he had a very good point!

The Headmaster had thoughtfully indicated, back at my initial interview, that he envisaged one would stay in one's first post between three and five years. When one felt it was time to move on one should feel no embarrassment at wishing to do so and he would be pleased to supply a supportive reference. This, of course, had the merit, from the school's point of view, of keeping salaries down, while ensuring a supply of young masters who would, like me, be happy to live in as bachelors and (not like me!) supervise games and outdoor activities! But it was also very sensible from the point of view of one's own career. One young master had recently moved on to Eton and another to Harrow, so in my fourth year I felt encouraged to start applying to larger schools, in spite of being perfectly happy in my post at St Lawrence, with a supportive and forward-looking Head of Department - who was to spend his entire career at St Lawrence ending up as Headmaster - and a very nice married Housemaster, for whom I acted as resident House Tutor. He also spent the rest of his career at St Lawrence, after his first post at his old school, Magdalen College School, Oxford - which was to be my last teaching post! The three of us were Oxford men and we liked to drive out after evening school and before dinner for a beer or two in the Brown Jug pub, on the road to Broadstairs at the infelicitously-named Dumpton Park. Of course, these days leaving the House unattended for an hour would be quite unthinkable! On one windy evening, as we returned a little boisterously through the Masters' Entrance for Dinner, I managed to put my arm through a glass panel in the door as the wind blew it back on me. Fortunately, no harm was done to me, but the atmosphere in the Masters' Dining Room was icy in the extreme when we entered, slightly flushed. "I'm afraid" I've put my arm through a pane in the door, I explained to the silent Second Master, who presided at the end of one table with one of the bachelor Housemasters on each side of him. "So we heard'" came the grim reply! Conversation proved difficult over the dinner table that evening.

As far as supervision duties go, things were quite relaxed, compared to today's rigorous requirements. Since all five boarding houses were in the one building, I suppose it was felt that one Duty Master on duty for the whole school could cover any legal liability, although individual houses also made their own duty arrangements. I ran the school's Film Society, which showed a movie most Saturday evenings for all boarders. This took place in the Taylor Hall, newly built in 1964 and already demolished now to make way for a girls' boarding house! There's also a new theatre. Back in the Sixties, House televisions were unknown, although one Housemaster did allow select groups of boys to watch the large television in his study some evenings.

As well as being in charge of the Hall on film evenings I was also usually in charge of Manor House. Since most boys attended the film this didn't usually give rise to any problems. However, one particular Saturday I received an urgent message in the Hall that a boy had fallen in the house and broken his wrist, so he needed to be taken to hospital. What to do? I had a reliable boy projectionist on our 16mm machine, but could I leave a potentially riotous assembly of some 300 boys alone at the film? I decided I had no choice but to put the boy into a taxi by himself and send him off alone to A & E. These days one would probably get reported by the hospital or an enraged parent for such action!

My usual duties in the House involved being present on my duty evenings, roughly two in the week and most weekends, while the married Housemaster remained with his family in his house down College Road. In the evenings I used to check that boys were settled down to Prep and then supervise their bedtimes, going round the dormitories at Lights Out and bidding them Good Night. In the winter months I found it necessary to wear my overcoat on my rounds of the spartan dormitories, and I pitied the boys in their pyjamas with the dormitory windows open the regulation six inches. Discipline was never usually a problem with two prefects allocated to each dormitory. However, on one occasion, a boy was marched into my study by a prefect who had caught him peeing out of the dormitory window. (The reader may recall that junior boys were required to go down two floors to the quad to relieve themselves.) Since I knew the Housemaster to be unavailable I was forced to punish the unfortunate boy by giving him 'six of the best' on the posterior with the Housemaster's cane, under the eye of the duty Prefect, who had insisted that this was the usual punishment. I found it a humiliating experience for both of us and it was the last time that I allowed myself to be driven into administering corporal punishment.

Although prefects were no longer allowed to administer any corporal punishment at St Lawrence the time-honoured public school tradition of fagging lingered on. Personal fagging- junior boys waiting on prefects in their studies, cleaning their shoes and so on- had been officially abolished, but it persisted on a house basis for chores around the Common Room, and such tasks. To this end 'Fagging Lists' were posted on the House notice boards. This caused astonishment and consternation to an American boy who had joined the College and been confronted with the lists of fags, American slang having given the word a rather particular meaning! Local usage had to be quickly explained to him before he rang his parents. In those pre-internet and pre-mobile phone times lonely boarders were dependent on the house telephone with its coin box for home calls, which were not encouraged. There was an exeat weekend roughly every three weeks, either side of half term. But the shorter Spring term had no half term break.

Towards the end of my time at St Lawrence, Saturday evenings were getting rather more difficult. I have vivid memories of drunken boys being carried back to the school by their companions in crime! Senior boys were allowed out on leave, but drinking was, of course, forbidden. Illicit smoking was another problem in those days too. It often led to a small fire being discovered in some cosy smokers' hideaway, when a cigarette had not been properly extinguished. Mercifully, drugs were still almost unknown back in those years, although I discovered when I met up with some old boys that they had been smoking cannabis. One always found these things out after they had left, which was just as well! I'm sorry to recall that one of the boys concerned later got very heavily into drugs at his Oxford college and sadly ended up in jail. I'm still in touch with one of his friends and contemporaries who was Captain of Rugger but also a great rebel. He belonged to Courtenay House, which was presided over by a wizened bachelor who taught Spanish and was Head of Modern Languages. This housemaster had conceived such a dislike of the Headmaster that he wouldn't face in his direction at Common Room meetings, but turned his corner chair to face away! You could almost say the whole of his House was in a state of rebellion. It was certainly a thorn in the Headmaster's side, having been formed after the war when a failed school called Courtenay had joined the College as a unit. This House was its legacy. Eventually the subversive Housemaster was edged out and the house was taken over by a grim Evangelical imported from somewhere up North who only lasted a year or so before he was replaced by a married housemaster who had joined the Common Room with me.

Another former pupil of mine at St Lawrence, Hugh Anderson, went on to Cambridge and eventually became President of the Cambridge Union. He very kindly invited me up to dine and attend any debate I wished, I arranged to attend the debate he had arranged with Enoch Powell as the main speaker. It was extremely interesting to be able to talk to such a controversial figure informally over dinner and then to hear him holding his own during the

Debate. There was a mob baying for Mr Powell's blood outside the Union Society building and he confided in me that he wondered how much longer he could face such unpleasant scenes. Things haven't changed, with some of our present politicians, like Amber Rudd, recently facing 'cancel culture' at universities. One would hope that educated people could at least give people with whom they disagree the right to a hearing. Very sadly, Hugh died young, as a result of a brain tumour. There was some speculation that it might have caused by his being struck by a cricket ball during a match. So I suppose the modern helmets worn by most cricketers are a sensible precaution, although they were sadly far too late for Hugh.

A pleasant feature of Manor House's intake during my time was a number of Persian, or Iranian boys. They were usually sophisticated and charming and I enjoyed dropping in on them in their studies for a thick Turkish-type coffee. The Housemaster was also often presented by them with pots of Beluga Caviar at the beginning of term. The 'boys' seemed very mature for their supposed age: under eighteen. They were rumoured to keep their packets of Disque Bleu cigarettes in their underpants, but that was something I was not prepared to investigate. It was difficult to establish their real ages because they used the Islamic calendar, but the fees at St Lawrence were significantly lower than at the Regency Language School in the town and I wondered if this was a factor in their choice of St Lawrence's Sixth Form in which to perfect their English.

I was delighted to be told by an Iranian boy who joined my last school, Magdalen College School in Oxford, that his father had been one of that group of boys in Manor during my time. I found out later that his father had actually become the leader of the Opposition in Iran before being imprisoned. A few years ago I was delighted to meet his son again, quite by chance, on the train from London back to Oxford. I was introduced to his wife and baby and reassured that his father was now safe.

We also had a very mature Head of House during my last year at St Lawrence, who was promoted as Head of School with his own study on the ground floor near the Masters' Dining room. I wasn't entirely surprised to discover, after he had left school, that he had been conducting an illicit affair with a local girl who lived conveniently close to the College in a semi up near the railway station. Apparently he had been a frequent guest overnight in her bedroom!

St Lawrence was famous as a Hockey-playing school during the Lent Term. Not only had the Head been a Hockey International and a Cambridge Blue, but the Housemaster of Tower, another cleric who also acted as Assistant Chaplain, was one of the founders of the Public Schools' Hockey Festival, held at each year at the beginning of the Easter Vacation in Oxford. In the Michaelmas Term at St Lawrence Rugby Football was the game. Perhaps because Hockey was THE school game, rebels were attracted to Rugger as a kind of protest. During my time the school was doing rather better at it than at Hockey. And when a plan was hatched to replace Rugger with extra hockey matches the Rugger results got even better in protest! There were certain matches that acquired an almost totemic importance, like the annual match against King's School, Canterbury. For this match attendance was required of the whole school, in order to support the First XV. All those boys not actually playing in matches were lined up alongside the pitch and a roll-call was taken. In front of the massed ranks, just over the touchline, would stand the Headmaster. And, on the opposite side of the field, would stand the Headmaster of King's, Canon 'Fred' Shirley, urging on his side. It was indeed a battle of the Titans! The two clerical Headmasters used also to exchange pulpits about once a year. Canon Shirley was notorious because, on moving from Worksop College to King's in 1935, he had 'poached' around 30 of its best boys and some masters and brought them south with him. For this his membership of the Headmasters' Conference had been suspended for a period. King's, at that time back in the Thirties, had been close to bankruptcy and Shirley had transformed its fortunes in some 30 years of Headship. He claimed it was the oldest public school in Britain, but St Peter's York also made that claim.

Another friend of mine in the Common Room who didn't really fit into the prim Evangelical background of St Lawrence was Patrick MacFarlan, the Head of History. He was also a bachelor, with a study opposite our Dining Room and a bedroom up on the top floor in Grange House territory, just along from my study. Patrick was a more subtle rebel than the Housemaster of Courtenay, and he made a point of befriending and encouraging green young masters like me. He had a great love of Venice, and I spent many evenings with him drinking some of his excellent wine under a lovely modern painting of Venice that hung in a corner of his study. He harboured a secret resentment that he had never been offered a Housemastership and attributed this to his lack of Evangelical sympathies. He was a proud Scotsman and, like me, a follower of the Jacobites and the House of Stuart. It was suggested to me by others that his being viewed as unsuitable for a House dated back to the time when he ran a school Poetry Society. The boy reciting a poem would hold a rose, which he then passed on to the next reciter. This was deemed to be unsuitable for adolescent boys, I was told! And so his card was marked. He had memorably played Feste in a legendary production of *Twelfth Night* in the open air theatre that used to be situated outside the Common Room. When I began to pursue a call to ordination in the Church of England, towards the end of my time at my next school, Harrow, Patrick revealed that he himself had once been a candidate for ordination, at Westcott House, Cambridge, along with his fellow Scotsman Patrick Rodger, who, as Bishop of Oxford, was eventually to ordain me in 1995.

The former Head of English was Housemaster of Lodge House, right at the top of the five storey main school building. He was a strong Evangelical and a mountain climber. He was in charge of the College's regular fire drills, when he would delight in abseiling down the outside of the building in a harness that formed one of the escape devices found on the higher floors. He insisted on his degrees being listed in the school diary and prospectus as 'B.A., M.A,' on the grounds that they were awarded respectively by two different universities- Cambridge and a rather dubious Evangelical establishment in the States called the Bob Jones University. He did not get on with my friend the Head of History who thought him an insufferable prig. On one notable occasion, after the Housemaster had made a particularly complacent remark during teatime, my friend simply rose and poured his cup of tea over the poor man's head in the middle of the Common Room!

Afternoon Tea was a great feature of Common Room life at St Lawrence. At 3.45pm or thereabouts a large trolley was wheeled into the Common Room laden with plates of sandwiches, bread and butter and a selection of tempting home-baked cakes, as well as the ubiquitous tea urn. Much as I enjoyed this, I don't think it did the health of the Common Room much good. There were a number of very well-upholstered masters, especially some of the resident bachelors! Notable amongst these was Tom, my predecessor as House Tutor of Manor, who could be seen leading his diminutive tribe of eleven year old boys up from Cameron House, while wielding a large shepherd's crook! In the winter it reminded me of Good King Wenceslas and his pageboys! Tom gave me some interesting driving advice when I mentioned that I found the M2 and the long Thanet Way which followed it made me prone to sleepiness. "I just go faster then," was his robust advice as he swept out in his large Austin Westminster saloon.

Ramsgate itself was still rather run-down in the Sixties. There were some elegant Regency terraces above the harbour, but they were in dire need of rescue. There were, however, some excellent junk shops ('antique' is too grand a description) where I picked up Regency chairs, tables and cupboards to pep up the institutional school furniture in my rooms. I even re-covered an armchair myself and repainted my study a tasteful shade of brown.

Ramsgate seafront was dominated by its harbour, which at that time received regular shipments of Volkswagen cars from Bremerhaven. Past a line of amusement arcades and cafes lay the bathing beach. In the other direction, on the West Cliff, was a fine Victorian Gothic Catholic church by the notable architect Augustus Welby Pugin. I found the services there a welcome change from the hearty Chapel services at the College and used to sneak down from time to time. The Grange, the house Pugin built for himself, was just nearby. In recent times both buildings have been restored to their former glory.

Further on lay Pegwell Bay, a shallow inlet on the estuary of the River Stour. It was probably the scene of both Roman invasions of Britain by Julius Caesar. In 2017 the University of Leicester excavated a large fort dating from 54 BC. The first Anglo-Saxon landings in Britain subsequently took place there around 450 AD. A few centuries later nearby Ebbsfleet was the scene of St Augustine's landing in 597 to convert Britain to Christianity at the behest of Pope Gregory the Great. From 1969 it was also the site of Britain's first purpose-built Hoverport, with a regular Hovercraft service across the Channel. Unfortunately this came just too late for me to, since I moved on to Harrow School in Autumn 1969.

Chapter Five

Stet Fortuna Domus

Harrow School

In 1968-9, my fourth year at St Lawrence, I decided to follow the Headmaster's advice when he appointed me and start applying to larger schools- but without the dubious help of Gabbitas-Thring this time! I tried a number of well-known establishments, including Harrow School, and was delighted to be summoned for interview at Harrow at the beginning of the Lent Term.

Harrow School 'Bill'

Having been born in Pinner, Middlesex, just a few miles from Harrow Hill, I was familiar with the school on the Hill's impressive buildings. Indeed, when my mother was a patient in the old Harrow Hospital on one side of the Hill,

I had made a habit of calling in to visit her on my way back from school in Hammersmith, by getting off the Piccadilly line train from school at South Harrow Station and walking up Roxeth Hill to the hospital. After my visit I would continue along the top of the Hill, past all the boarding houses and the straw-hatted Harrovians sauntering along the High Street, towards Church Hill and the descent to Harrow-on-the-Hill Metropolitan line station and a train back to Pinner or Eastcote stations. On occasion I stopped off at one of the Hill's little tea shops, patronized by boisterous groups of well-spoken boys. How I envied them, compared to my drab commuting life from Eastcote to Ravenscourt Park station each day!

So it was exciting to find myself ringing the bell at the Head Master's imposing house along the High Street, opposite the little road that ran up to St Mary's Church on the top of the Hill, notably described as "The Church Visible" by Queen Elizabeth I. In due course, I was admitted by a solemn grey-haired man who informed me he was the Head Master's Secretary, and shown into a very impressive drawing room, with magnificent views over London, spread out beyond and below the gardens and the school estate. The Head Master, Dr R. L. James, soon entered and conducted me to his Study along the hallway. This was another impressively large room, with comfortable seating and a desk in one corner. A fire burnt in the fireplace, with a fender around it. I was soon put at my ease by the Head Master, who latched on to the fact that I had been a boy at Latymer Upper School. He told me he had been a master at our great rival, St Paul's School, before the war and had returned in peacetime as High Master before moving to Harrow in 1953. I didn't tell him that we Latymerians used to amuse ourselves by chanting "Balls to Paul's" when we saw their Eights on the river. Instead, we reminisced about our charismatic Head at Latymer, 'Freddie' Wilkinson. Dr James, whose affectionate nickname amongst masters, family and friends, I discovered later, was 'Jimmy,' remarked that they had been getting worried at St Paul's over Latymer's increasing academic success, rivalling the more eminent St Paul's in the number of Oxbridge Awards it was obtaining throughout the Fifties. We chatted amicably, over gin and tonics, but he did most of the talking, which I feared might not be a good omen for the outcome of the interview.

Soon it was time for lunch, and I was bidden to follow the Head Master through his own imposing Dining Room with its green baize double door into the boys' side of the house, and down one flight of stairs to the boys' House Dining Room. Inside, there was a central table with tables on either side. Dr James took his place at the head of this table and motioned me to a seat halfway along one side, with senior boys on either side and opposite me. Now came *my* chance to talk, and the boys were interesting and good at drawing me out. From time to time I caught sight of the Head Master's beady eye at his end of the table, observing our animated conversation. It began to dawn on me that this was a clever way to see if potential beaks would fit into the school.

After coffee, back in the Head Master's drawing room, and a brief introduction to his wife, always known as 'Bobbie,' since she loathed her Christian name Maud, I was free to make my way back down to Ramsgate, with a promise from the Head Master that he would be in touch. I was surprised that I had not met the Head of English or any other masters, but I assumed this would come later, if my application was pursued. Lent Term went on at St Lawrence with the usual miserable weather and no news

67

from Harrow. I tried one or two other applications without enthusiasm, since I had decided Harrow was the school to which I really wanted to move.

As the end of term at St Lawrence approached I was summoned by Canon Perfect, who explained that he would be retiring at the end of the Summer Term, so it was important to know if I would be staying on at St Lawrence. He didn't want to leave his successor short of an English master. I replied that I was still awaiting news from Harrow and it was clear to me that the Canon thought that was a forlorn hope. I discovered later that he hadn't even been approached for a reference by Dr James! A few days before the end of term, just as I'd almost resigned myself to staying on at St Lawrence, I received a telegram: "Offer in post. James!" Dr James's letter offering me the job duly arrived and I accepted with alacrity, sad as I was to be leaving St Lawrence after my happy years there. I was a bit worried about not giving them more notice to fill my place, until I discovered my Head of Department had provisionally lined up a former pupil, just completing his English degree at Oxford, to take over from me should I get another job! So everyone was happy! I later discovered that the probable reason for Dr James' delay in offering me the Harrow job was that he was contemplating appointing his elder son, who had been teaching in a prep school, to the Harrow job! Fortunately for me, he had decided not to run the risk of being accused of nepotism!

As my last summer term at St Lawrence wore on, my thoughts turned to the question of accommodation at Harrow. All masters were required to reside in school accommodation on the Hill, but what would that be like? Eventually a letter arrived from Dr James, explaining that he wanted to discuss a possibility with me and inviting me up to the School again. After some pleasant preliminary chatter, he explained that there were no resident House Tutors as yet at Harrow and that bachelors generally lived in 'colonies' of three or so, sharing unfurnished flats provided by the school. Perhaps he read my look of dismay, since he proceeded to offer another possibility. I could lodge on the private side of the Head Master's House, taking breakfast and dinner with him and his wife. Lunch would be taken, as I had already experienced, with the House. On occasions when the James's had to give a dinner party I would be able to have a tray up in my room, which was to be on the first floor. No doubt I would be able to help in the House on an informal basis, although there was also a resident Housemaster who was responsible for the day to day running of the House.

Naturally, I was delighted with this proposal and accepted it with alacrity. There was still no opportunity offered to meet the Head of English! Fortunately my former colleague at St Lawrence, who had preceded me to Harrow, in his case to teach Chemistry, had mentioned my appointment to his English colleague, who wrote me a very nice note. My appointment was apparently news to him, but he was glad to have an addition to his Department and he was arranging for me to teach the Classical Remove, which comprised the brightest new boys, and a full timetable up to A Level. I learnt later that the History master who had usually taught that form English was rather miffed at being supplanted by a new master, or 'beak,' as Harrow teachers are known, but he got it back after my first year. I am still in touch with two Old Harrovians from that form. One is vicar of a South London parish, and the other, who became Head of School, became the lay Administrator of the Catholic Shrine of Our Lady at Walsingham. Not all Harrovians have had such religious careers, although at least another two are bishops! At one point I found myself teaching four earls, mostly for remedial English! I needn't have worried about not having an English degree. I found there was only one member of the English Department who had one, and he soon left to become a Headmaster!

After spending a delightful final summer term down at St Lawrence, come September I was ready to start a new chapter at Harrow. Dr James had been vague as to when I was expected, but I decided I had better not leave it later than the day before term started. When I duly turned up at the front door I was met by a slightly surprised Head Master, who took me in, but explained there would be no need for me to turn up any earlier than the actual start of term in future.

My room on the first floor of the grand house was opposite the Head Master's Secretary's office, just along from the James' own bedroom. Early in my stay I encountered my employer crossing the passage clad only in his pyjama top crossing to his own bathroom! He let out a yelp and leapt inside! From the window over my bed I had a panoramic view past Wembley stadium to the high rise blocks of the City and the dome of St Paul's with its cross catching the sun. There was a bathroom across the passage, next door to the Secretary's office, and I was informed it was for my use. It was also used by Sappho, the James' ancient terrier! She was usually quiescent in her basket, but – not being any kind of dog-lover since I was knocked down as a small boy by a neighbour's dog - I opened the door gingerly when I needed to visit the bathroom. I always felt particularly vulnerable when stepping naked out of the bath! Turning left out of my room, there was a door that led to the servants' stairs and it was tactfully suggested to me that, if

I had any boys to visit me, I should ask them to use these stairs, which linked with the boys' side of the house. I always felt a little uncomfortable using the main staircase myself, especially if I had a guest with me. Certainly, if it was late at night, I found it best to use the servants' staircase. It was also a convenient route to the butler's pantry, where I collected my dinner tray on evenings when there was a grand dinner-party, with Herbert the butler in his tails. The menu was often the same on these occasions: soup, followed by a large turkey and then a delicious concoction of ginger biscuits and cream for dessert. The wine was always from Berry Bros and Rudd, in St James. Dr James would come into the Pantry with opened bottles to let them breathe before evening school. On Sunday evenings the preacher at Evensong usually came to dinner and I was welcome on such occasions, when I would make myself useful by handing the vegetables round, in the absence of any servants.

Breakfast with one's employer and his wife every day might sound rather taxing; but, in practice, it was a pleasant occasion. After cereal one helped oneself to bacon and eggs, etc. from the chafing dish and settled down to read the newspaper that Dr James had asked me to order for myself, since we didn't talk at breakfast, except on Sundays when three or four bachelor masters would join us. Mrs James had found some of them wandering around looking rather lost on a Sunday morning and decided to invite groups of them into Sunday breakfast. Not all of them were delighted with this well-meant invitation!

After breakfast and a perusal of *The Daily Telegraph* (to which I had converted the Head Master from *The Times,* which had increasingly annoyed him with its 'pinkish' views) Dr James would make his way in cap and gown towards the School Chapel, past the Vaughan Memorial Library. It was impressive to see the way the ranks of Harrovians parted in front of his small but authorative figure as he progressed along the pavement. On Saturday mornings, as at St Lawrence, the short morning service would be replaced by a Hymn Practice, conducted by the Director of Music or his Assistant. As I prepared to make my way along to it I encountered Dr James, who informed me that, although he had to attend to ensure discipline, there was no need for beaks to inflict it upon themselves!

Boys sat in house blocks in Chapel and their attendance was discreetly checked by the house monitors from the list of names at the end of each pew. Should a boy be tempted to converse in Chapel the standard punishment was 200 Double, or lines. Dr James' successor told the beaks that he had no objection to their allowing boys 'quiet conversation' before the service began. Unfortunately this civilized rule soon led to such an increase in the volume of noise before Custos (the school porter) pressed the bell to signal to the waiting Chaplain down in the vestry that all was in order for his entrance that one might well have been in a theatre awaiting Curtain Up!

There was usually an intake of new boys each term and they would turn up the evening before term started with their parents, who would be entertained modestly with a glass of sherry by the Head Master before a sometimes tearful farewell to their son, who would be ushered through to the boys' side of the House. I write 'side,' but in reality the boys' quarters were on either side of the Head Master's residence, linked by a subterranean passage through the kitchens and staff quarters. One side of boys' rooms - most boys had their own, except for the youngest - had been added in the Victorian era and was known as the 'New' side. There was also the 'New New' side, which referred to two floors which Dr James had arranged for a local builder to add on top of the original building on the other side of his quarters. When, towards the end of my time at Harrow, I became a local Councillor and sat on the Council's Development Control Committee I learnt that the Planning Department had viewed the ad hoc nature of the School's recent new buildings with some surprise. I used to enjoy the occasional cup of tea with the House Matron in her room situated below the new floors in the Head Master's and she used to point to ominous cracks in the wall, caused – she was convinced - by the additional weight above! She said it gave her sleepless nights!

New masters could be given a rough ride by Harrovians. I well remember one early gaffe I made, in casually remarking that these days we were all middle class. I was left in no doubt that most of the form did NOT consider themselves to be 'middle class!' Obstreperous boys were not the only obstacle one met. There were certain colleagues who could be extremely unwelcoming: in particular, three of the senior housemasters. I crossed swords with one of them, who was mostly interested in cricket but taught some science as well, after taking a party of boys to the theatre in London and getting back to the Hill a little later than anticipated. I had to deal with his very irate wife on the telephone and my request to discuss the matter instead with my colleague, the housemaster, was NOT well received! There was another housemaster, an Old Harrovian, who was also a noted cricketer, who taught English and Latin to lower forms. He was notorious for having - and using - a nickname for every boy he taught. He and another Old Harrovian housemaster, who taught Geography, had apparently decided that I was sexually ambivalent. At a beaks' party they ganged up against me and, pushing themselves against the wall, they exclaimed,

"Look out! Here's one of these Rattigan fellows- keep your back to the wall!" They had both been boys at the school with the distinguished Old Harrovian playwright Terence Rattigan. Embarrassing as their "welcome" to a new colleague was, I decided it was best shrugged off and, indeed, a few years later I was accepted into their reactionary circle! I was told then that, as a new master, I hadn't been expected to last more than a year or so!

I suppose one reason for the reception I met from some colleagues was what they may have regarded as my privileged position as a member of the Head Master's household. This meant that at evening events in Speech Room, such as the Lady Bourchier Speaking Competition, I would be invited to join the Head Master's party and be greeted by the School rising to their feet as our party, in Black Tie and gowns for Dr James and myself, made our way to our allocated seats. Colleagues would also have been aware that I had the Head Master's ear at his table, although, of course, I tried to avoid 'shop' and would never have dreamt of discussing a colleague with the Head Beak! Not even those two outrageous housemasters!

I was reminded of all that, buried in past memory, very recently when I was telephoned in my retirement flat in Oxford by the Labour candidate for the forthcoming Council elections. I told him I had only ever voted Conservative and had indeed served as a Conservative Councillor in the London Borough of Harrow. This led him into confessing that he had been at school at Harrow. I asked him if he meant Harrow School and he reluctantly admitted it, adding that, as a Labour candidate, he didn't normally like it to be known! This led us on to a pleasant conversation about the School. He said there were some terrible masters and teaching! See above! He told me he had been there in the early Sixties - a few years prior to my time. So *I* was in the clear! I did say that I thought the Head of English was a brilliant teacher and he agreed, as he had been taught by him. He also agreed when I said how very kind Dr James had been- especially to me as a new beak. But I had to agree with him about those two dreadful old housemasters. He mentioned another one, who had already retired when I joined the school, but of whom I had heard much. On one occasion boys had managed to lower an enormous fish in front of the blackboard, unnoticed by him while he was holding forth! After he had retired, he used to revisit the Hill and sneak back into the House over which he had presided through the boys' entrance, without the courtesy of asking the current Housemaster for his permission. In this way he did a nice job of undermining his successor!

On Monday mornings, instead of Chapel, the whole school would assemble in Speech Room so that notices could be given out and any special arrangements for the coming week announced. On the platform the Head Master was flanked on either side by the six most senior masters. One's position in the list of masters and boys - the Bill book - was strictly determined by seniority at that time. I remember being very exercised about my own position in the list, which hinged upon the exact date of my appointment.

There was a memorable occasion when we all entered Speech Room to find a motorbike suspended above the Head Master's table on the platform. We awaited his arrival with baited breath. But he didn't turn a hair. He just carried on as normal. It was a notable example of Jimmy's sang-froid! On another occasion every seat from the boys' and beaks' chairs had been removed. We all perched uncomfortably on the frames of our seats and again the proceedings carried on as if there was nothing amiss. I suspect undercover investigations followed, but we heard no more about these jeux d'esprit.

Methods of enforcing classroom discipline were strictly circumscribed. The traditional punishment for miscreants was called 'Double.' This involved a boy being set to copy out a certain number of lines - usually in units of one hundred - of Latin hexameters or English blank verse. To ensure that their handwriting didn't expand to fill the paper the lines had to be copied on specially ruled paper, which determined the top and bottom of the letters - hence 'Double,' since the lines were ruled in pairs. This paper had to be obtained from a boy's housemaster, so a check could be kept on miscreants - and also on those masters who were reduced too often to setting such punishments!

Corporal punishment was still in use, but only by monitors - who had to get their housemaster's permission, or at least write their reason in a special book - and by housemasters themselves. Individual beaks were not allowed to beat boys.
Other punishments, usually inflicted by monitors, involved runs, usually early in the morning. Dr James confided in me that he had been put under some pressure by his fellow Heads at their annual conference to stop boys beating other boys, but he rebutted their pleas, declaring that he wouldn't be told how to run his school by others. Indeed, he and a few like-minded Headmasters would often absent themselves from some of the more tedious sessions on the Conference programmes to get together in some convivial setting.

There was still one house where cold early morning baths -'toshes' as they were called - were the rule, but this was not the case in the Head Master's. Indeed I learned from the boys when I undertook house duties that one boy was rumoured to have avoided bathing for a whole term! There were no showers in the boys' houses in those days and the 'toshes' were few and far between.

Houses varied in character and heartiness, reflecting both tradition and individual housemasters' interests. So The Knoll, Newlands and The Grove were civilized houses and harboured many boys with artistic inclinations. The Head Master's was one of the largest houses and it tended to be very mixed in tone. Certainly there were boys whose school family pedigree stretched back seven generations, as Jimmy pointed out to me on the House boards, on which all new boys' names were carved. But there were also many first generation boys. The housemaster encouraged civilized and relaxed attitudes to games. But woe betide such a boy if he found himself misplaced in West Acre or The Park!

Dr James allowed individual housemasters considerable latitude in the way in which they chose to run their houses. Before the Second World War housemasters had even been permitted to run their houses for profit, making what they could on catering and staff bills. In 1969 it was still their responsibility to hire and pay domestic staff. Should there be a walkout by the staff, it was up to the Housemaster and his wife, if he had one, to cover- so there were a number of housemasters' wives or matrons who had horrendous tales of having been faced in an emergency with cooking lunch for 70 hungry boys and masters.

Only two houses still employed proper butlers, who presided at house lunch as well as acting as butler for the housemaster on the private side. In the Grove, there was Harry, a model of slightly prissy dignity, and in the Head Master's we had Herbert. On the private side of the house we also had Violet, an aged housemaid who suffered 'turns' at every full moon. She brought my early morning tea up to my room, except on her day off, when the Polish au pair would substitute. It was always a bit embarrassing when I met the au pair after she had married the House Tutor, who subsequently became Housemaster of another House. Before the war, the Head Master had employed two footmen as well as a butler, so Jimmy told me. He also pointed out that fees at schools like Harrow in those days were frequently much higher than at more run-of-the-mill public schools, whereas now there was a much narrower margin between schools' fees. He strove hard to keep fees to a level that professional people could still afford.

There were still some houses that were run in the old style, where the monitors ruled the roost. After House Prayers, which followed Prep, the boys lined up to shake hands and say "Good-night" to the Housemaster and his wife and House Tutor, if there was one. After that, house discipline was left entirely to the monitors in the more traditional houses. Dr James used to enjoy visiting boys in his House in their studies for a natter, as he put it. In this way he was able to keep his ear to the ground unobtrusively. On many evenings after dinner Bobbie would leave us at the table and we would converse until Jimmy announced he was off round the House, through the green baize door from his Dining Room. It was through that same door that his distinguished Victorian predecessor Dr Vaughan had gone to visit a pupil of whom he had become too fond, as Jimmy liked to recall. Vaughan was forced by the boy's parents to resign from Harrow and it was some time before he was allowed, as a clergyman, to quietly accept a Deanery.

Jimmy's own father had been Dean of Bangor in the Church in Wales. When a book was published detailing Dr Vaughan's misbehaviour, Dr James was telephoned by the Press for his reaction. "Oh, we've put the book in the Vaughan Memorial Library," was his splendidly insouciant reply. It was typical of his method of dealing with the press, whom he regarded with suspicion. If they telephoned they would encounter a warning message that the conversation was being recorded. If they arrived on the Hill without an invitation they would be swiftly told to depart before the Police were called. I think this steely attitude may have been encouraged by an item that appeared in the well-known journalist John Gordon's column in the *Sunday Express* after Dr James was caught speeding, while driving back from a masonic dinner with two of his housemasters. Gordon made much of the modest fine that was awarded, as against a much higher one handed out to an 'ordinary' citizen.

Dr James was 67 when he retired as Head Master, having been invited by the Governors to stay on for Harrow's 400th year, when Her Majesty the Queen would be the guest of honour. It would be her second visit to the school with Dr James in charge. On the morning of the great day Jimmy came down to breakfast looking grim. "That sh*t Mortimer!" he hissed through clenched teeth. John Mortimer, the Old Harrovian author and lawyer, was no fan of his old school.
He had been interviewed on the breakfast programme on the wireless that morning about Harrow's Quatercentenary celebrations. Mortimer had made derogatory comments about the school and suggested that your typical Old Harrovian would be a secondhand car salesman in suede shoes!

When it came to arrangements for the royal visit, Dr James was quite clear that Her Majesty wanted to meet boys, rather than masters. She was friends with some of the boys' parents and a couple at least had acted as her pages. (One of these a few years later set fire to his House, excusing himself to the Police by claiming that he had been molested by another boy.) Reverting to arrangements for the great day, I was told that my bathroom would be put aside for the Queen's use during her visit, and Dr James joked that as a supporter of the Jacobites it might be necessary to lock me up during the visit! This didn't happen, and I am in a position to confirm that a white calf-covered seat had been sent from the Palace and installed in time for the visit and collected afterwards!

I have always been a strong believer in the educational value of school debating, having first found my feet as a speaker at the Freston (Debating) Society at my old school, Latymer Upper. I had continued this interest by speaking in the Union Society at Oxford and polishing my technique by attending the Speakers' Classes organized by the Oxford University Conservative Association. So it was natural that Dr James should consider me to be the man to revive Sixth Form Debating at Harrow. One of the problems of the separate Houses was that boys tended to get so comfortable in them in the evenings that it was difficult to tempt them out into the rather austere surroundings of the Old Harrovians' Room in the War Memorial Building, which was the venue for inter-house meetings of this kind. It struck me that an inducement might be necessary to encourage attendance, so I suggested to Dr James that we provide port. "Cheap port is revolting," was his outspoken reply, "you'd better serve Madeira." So we complied with the Headmagisterial decree and attendances accordingly picked up.

The General Election of 1970 came at a difficult time in Britain's history. The Wilson government had failed to rein in trade union power and there were frequent strikes. It was generally felt that we were a nation in decline. Jimmy announced that he would watch the results on television and invited me to join him. When Edward Heath's surprise victory became clear by the early hours of the morning we opened a bottle of champagne! Next autumn Mr Heath was the Guest of Honour at Churchill Songs in Speech Room, an annual event which commemorates Winston Churchill's return visits to the Hill for Songs during the dark days of World War 2. After Songs, masters, their wives and selected guests were always invited back to the Head Master's for drinks. It was noticeable that Mr Heath felt he was out of his milieu and conversation was difficult. I was reminded of Heath's visit to St Lawrence some years prior, when he was asked if he had visited the College while he was a boy at Chatham House Grammar School, down in the town. He gave the impression of having a massive chip on his shoulder on that occasion too. A few years later the country was plunged into a miners' strike, with resulting power shutdowns.

Dr James' retirement meant that I had to move out of my room in the Head Master's house after two very happy years. I knew that I would miss his and Bobbie's company very much, as well as contact with the boys in the House at lunch and other times. I even contemplated moving on from Harrow at that stage, conscious that things would be very different for me in future. I was interviewed for Head of English posts at a public school in the Midlands and at an Oxfordshire grammar school. My father had developed Alzheimers and by 1970 he was having to spend most of his time as an in-patient in Littlemore Hospital, after he had tried to attack my mother at home. The James' were particularly kind about this, since they knew he could only come home if I were there to help and to collect him and take him back to hospital. Furthermore, Bobbie told me that one of her own parents had also developed Alzheimers, so she was particularly understanding. Tragically, after Jimmy had died at the age of 77, Bobbie herself went on to develop this horrid disease. I was told not to feel guilty about driving over to Oxford on Sundays in order to help my mother cope with my father. I used to dread the time on Sunday evenings when I had to take my father back to Littlemore Hospital and struggle to undress him and get him to bed in a room that had clearly once been a padded cell. We used to put off leaving home in North Oxford as late as possible, so I regularly didn't get back to Harrow until after midnight.

I eventually decided to withdraw from both the posts I had applied for, since I really didn't want to leave Harrow. The Headmaster of the Midlands school was clearly on the way out. I had noticed when he offered me a drink in his study before lunch that he had poured himself a very large amount of gin with his tonic! I mentioned this to Dr James, who drily observed that he had heard that the Headmaster was "rather tired." The Grammar School was about to become a Comprehensive and the old Head had assured me that he wouldn't be making any changes in the traditional way in which he ran the school. That didn't strike me as a very promising situation either!

Having turned down these posts and decided to stay on at Harrow I had to face up to looking after myself in school accommodation. Here again Dr James came to my rescue. My father died in Jimmy's last term as Head Master and, having met my mother, he decided he could let me have a small house to myself so she could come to stay. I think I was almost the first bachelor to be given his own accommodation, although later on the new Head Master, Michael Hoban, made flats available to the Chaplain and, later, to the Assistant Chaplain Peter Gamble.

Jimmy and Bobbie James retired to North Oxford, just a mile or two away from my mother's house, which made it very easy for me to keep in touch with them in their retirement. My mother was delighted to entertain them to dinner from time to time and found they had a lot in common. It was also a pleasure to see His Honour Judge Lawrence Verney again, when he and his wife Zoe came over to dinner from Buckinghamshire. I was able to keep Jimmy in touch with events on the Hill and hear his trenchant views on some of the changes, receiving more wise advice over the years. On one notable occasion he and Bobbie entertained His Majesty King Hussein of Jordan at their house, when his arrival to see his old Head Master, complete with security detail, certainly impressed the neighbours in the quiet North Oxford suburb!

On the Hill, as a bachelor, I found life outside the Head Master's rather lonely, having been used to being surrounded by colleagues and boys for my previous seven years in the teaching profession. My new life was not very different from teaching in a day school. To fill up my empty evenings I took an additional job in one of the local Further Education Colleges, housed in the former Commercial Travellers' School buildings up in Hatch End, Pinner. This involved teaching adults with literacy problems two evenings a week and I found it very rewarding. There were similar problems to those of my dyslexic earls at Harrow! But sadly I had to give it up after a year, since I found term dates didn't fit with Harrow's and there were also certain evening functions at the school which I needed to attend.

It didn't seem fair to my new pupils at Hatch End to be regularly having to miss their classes.

After this year I was able to swap my little school house in Crown Street for the penthouse flat above the London Steak House restaurant opposite the King's Head hotel that had been offered initially to the Chaplain. I found this a much more cheerful residence, with panoramic views in one direction towards Pinner and in the other towards London. I was also invited to help in the Head Master's as a non-resident House Tutor, so I was glad to be able to resume some pastoral house contacts. I started producing House plays, with the Housemaster and new Head Master's encouragement, so my evenings began to fill up again. Jimmy James had not been a great fan of drama, especially since he had reluctantly attended a performance of Shelagh Delaney's *A Taste of Honey* in the West End! He also complained that, since the Second World War, times of performances had been brought forward, leaving no time for a decent dinner beforehand.

Drama at Harrow in the Seventies was very much an ad hoc affair. There was no Head of Drama or a school theatre at that time. Speech Room was far from ideal for drama. For the annual Shakespeare Play a temporary structure that reproduced Shakespeare's stage at the Globe was erected early in the Summer Term. The Old Harrovian Players would give their own Shakespearian production a few weeks into term and then the school production would follow. Anyone who wanted to put on a house play had to work around these dates. It was possible to have a structure suspended from pulleys in the roof of Speech Room that provided the rudiments of a proscenium arch stage, but it was far from ideal. There were no dressing room facilities, so boys had to change in the War Memorial building and brave the open space between the two buildings in costume and make-up. The Music School had a small auditorium and occasionally house plays were presented there. That was a smaller and more intimate space, but again far from ideal and it depended on the willingness of the Director of Music to make it available. Additionally, when I came to produce Noel Coward's *Hay Fever*, I was up against the miners' strike and the Three Day Week! Rehearsals had to be fitted in to slots before the power cuts came.

More productions for the Head Master's and the Grove followed, culminating in my production of Peter Luke's dramatic adaptation of Frederick Rolfe's *Hadrian VII*. This fantasy imagined that another English Pope had been chosen at the end of the nineteenth century. I had seen the original production at the Mermaid Theatre and had been keen to do it ever since. Speech Room was a wonderful auditorium for dramatic processions of cardinals in full regalia (although Matron, pressed into service as Wardrobe Mistress, had baulked at coping with the six huge cardinals' trains that I had hired from the Birmingham Rep!) I also had the perfect boy actor, who had played the vampish Myra Arundel in *Hay Fever*, for the title role in *Hadrian*. I still treasure the memory of him seated on the great throne in Speech Room in his white papal soutane, insouciantly smoking a cigarette! I hasten to add that this was required in the text. A number of my friends who were very 'High Church' clergymen lent various props and attended the performances. We had to hire the papal tiara from Birmingham Rep, however! The journey to Birmingham and back to pick up all the costumes packed in a huge skip in the school minibus was a saga in itself. About ten years later, after I had been ordained as an Anglican clergyman, I was delighted to be invited to give the blessing at the 'Pope's' marriage and I'm pleased that I still see him from time to time at Old Harrovian dinners in London.

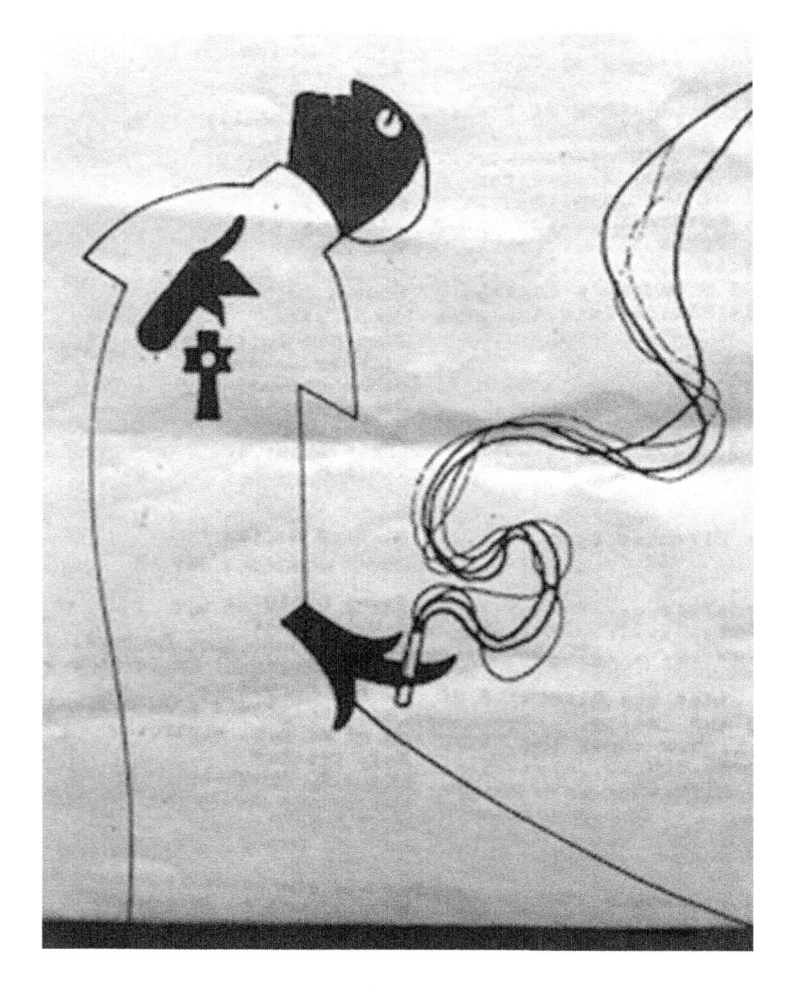

Hadrian VII

There was no masters' dining room at Harrow until the Shepherd Churchill Hall was built for central dining by all the houses in 1976, during Michael Hoban's headmastership. The School was forced to sell Shepherd Market, in the heart of Mayfair, to finance the project. This might seem a short-sighted decision, since it was said to be the School's only substantial property asset. However, it did have an upside, in that Shepherd Market was a notorious area for prostitution, as a stroll through it and a glance at the cards by the door bells would confirm. At the last minute there was a proposal to economize, by omitting the masters' dining facility! It was actually suggested that sandwiches might be provided instead in the basement of the War Memorial! I was on the committee set up by the Head Master, so I remember that tussle well! Another tussle came over making provision for the boys' straw hats, which they wore up to School. Since they would come straight into lunch from classes I pointed out that the cloakrooms would need to provide racks for all 750 hats. Reluctantly it was conceded. I suspect I had thwarted a plan to get rid of the famous Harrow hats by the back door, and my intervention didn't make me popular with the modernisers.

Before the Shepherd Churchill was built and boys lunched in their houses with their Housemaster and his wife and House Matron, it was very much a lottery as to whether a master got a free lunch. Unless one was officially attached to a house, as I was at the Head Master's, until Dr James' retirement, it was up to individual Housemasters to invite whom they pleased. If a beak's face fitted all well and good- but, even then, invitations were usually for one day a week only and for one term only. So a group of us younger masters used to eat in a local pub on the days for which we had no House lunch invitations. This could lead to a somnolent afternoon! Fortunately, in the two winter terms, lessons didn't start again until 5.15pm.

Michael Hoban was the last Head Master actually to live in the Head Master's House, until the most recent Head, four more on. He and his wife continued generously to entertain masters and their wives, but their style was very different from the James'. They had created a self-contained flat for themselves on the first floor of the Head Master's, with its own kitchen-diner. Dr and Mrs James never had a proper kitchen, making do with the old Butler's pantry for the odd drink or snack. I'm not sure how they managed during school holidays- I know Bobbie was no cook! Under the Hobans, entertainment usually took the form of buffet suppers, served in their old private dining room, whose grand furniture and chandeliers remained in situ. But there weren't enough seats for the numbers attending, so one perched wherever one could with one's plate. I remember one particular supper party when I was perched on the stairs outside the dining room and Herbert the butler passed me by, with a gently raised eyebrow. I couldn't resist calling out to him that I had eaten in various places in the Head Master's but never 'below stairs!' I noticed afterwards that my remark had unfortunately been overheard by the Head Master.

Whereas Dr James received regular deliveries from Berry Bros and Rudd, or Justerini and Brooks in St James, Michael Hoban favoured the local off licence. His wife Jasmine used to wheel her shopping trolley along the top of the Hill to the International stores for groceries, scandalizing some of the stuffier Housemasters' wives. So the new regime had a very different feel from the traditional one of Dr James. As his obituary in *The Times* in 1987 put it:
"He was not by nature an innovator and resisted the winds of change with persistence and relish."

One rather old-fashioned innovation that I was given permission by the new Head Master to preside over was the Alkmeonidae. This was a group of senior boys who elected new members to their club, rather in imitation of the old-established and all-powerful Pop at Eton. The Alkmeonidae had been dreamt up by a Sixth former in the Head Master's. He was a descendant of the father of the Scout movement, and his clever choice of a classical name for the club no doubt appealed to the new Head Master, who was a classicist, like his predecessor. There were around a dozen boys elected to the club, which usually met in my flat over cheese and wine. To prevent the boys drinking too much, I organized games of Consequences, which kept them occupied in thinking up unlikely combinations of names. The finished results, often hilarious, were then read out. I was always very careful to destroy the papers afterwards and make sure none left my flat.

Alkmeonidae 1974

One summer I decided it would be a good idea to take the Club punting on the River Cherwell in Oxford, as my home there was near the Cherwell Boathouse. As we drove down Norham Road towards my house the minibus dropped on one side and there was a horrible grinding noise. A wheel had come loose and was about to drop off! My consternation was matched only by my relief that this hadn't occurred as I was speeding along the M40. If it had, the consequences could have been very serious indeed. As it was, the local garage in the mews just round from my house was able to fix the wheel properly while my mother produced tea for the boys. The minibus had been serviced by the school's garage the previous week!

Once a year - or perhaps more often - we would dine, together with another master as our guest - usually a favourite housemaster of the boys - in a local restaurant. This was usually the Old Etonian, a cheekily named, but excellent French restaurant on the Hill. In time, a rival second club was founded by a group of boys who couldn't get themselves elected to the Alkmeonidae and therefore christened themselves the Dregs. I took pity on them and accepted their invitation to become their Senior Member as well. Unfortunately I heard they had been disbanded after I had left because of a drunken evening that culminated in being arrested in the middle of the High Street. I still have the ties of both societies, neither of which now exists.

Fines dinners were another pleasant social occasion. These were given by the monitors of a particular house and took place in the house dining room, with the permission of the Housemaster. Three or four masters would be invited as the house monitors' guests, I assume to ensure decorum. I have vivid memories of one particular dinner where guests were asked to turn up in fancy dress. The Head of English came as Margot Fonteyn, in a tutu and tights which did nothing for his generous proportions, while the Head of Classics, not the most muscular of men, attended as Rudolf Nureyev, also in tights. They arrived by taxi, professing to have heard nothing of the Head Master's last minute attempt to ban fancy dress.

Another master who employed a taxi was the Head of Modern Languages, who lived in a house, and taught in a form room, at the far end of the Hill from Speech Room. Head Master Hoban introduced a rule that all masters should attend Monday morning break in the Beaks' Room, up in the Old Harrovian Building, next to Speech Room. This was only a five minute walk along the High Street from the master in question's form room, but he duly ordered a taxi and arrived in style for break each week to make his point.

Harrow has its own unique collection of school songs, dating from the 1860s right up to recent times. They are still sung regularly at House Singings, as well as on grander occasions such as the annual Churchill Songs, commemorating Sir Winston's visits to his old school to sing them, from the darkest days of the Second World War onward. They are sung wherever Old Harrovians gather all around the world. Usually, a few guests - beaks and their wives - were entertained to dinner before a House Singing. A frequent guest in the Head Master's was His Honour Judge Verney, with his moving solo rendition of *You*, a song dating from the Boer War. Each song is introduced by a 'Put-on,' linking a certain group of people with a particular song for them to sing, such as all those who belonged to the Harrow School Corps to sing, *Left! Right!* or cricketers to sing, *A Gentleman's A-Bowling.* You get the idea. But sometimes boys' own 'put-ons' in the Houses could verge on the personal: *St Joles* for instance, who was "the friend of the lazy boy." Another traditional after-dinner entertainment that was still alive and kicking at The Park, under Charles and Margaret Laborde, was charades. Many innocent hours of fun were had in this way in the 1970s.

The official school society for the 'bloods' was the Philathletic Club and they had the privilege of wearing bow ties instead of the usual black or striped sports ties. They had their own room in the War Memorial Building, opposite the Monitors' Room. The Monitors had their own distinctive tie as well. On Sundays and special occasions tails were still worn by all boys for Chapel and formal events, with striped trousers, except for very small boys - of whom there were a diminishing number- who still wore 'bum freezers'- short, waist length jackets. There was also a plethora of sports ties, blazers, caps and pillboxes, including some with long tassels, like Victorian gentlemen's smoking hats, in all the colours of the rainbow. But the regular outfit for lessons was a plain navy blue flannel blazer -'bluer'- grey trousers and the shallow Harrow straw hat, often very battered and varnished. It was a hazard while walking around the form room to avoid putting one's foot through hats carelessly left on the floor. In my freezing 16th century form room at the back of the Old Schools, with one ancient heating pipe in a corner, we all used to keep our overcoats on and mittens came in useful, if one was writing on the blackboard. Later on, the English Department moved en masse into The Copse, a delightful neo-Georgian house down Grove Hill, past Speech Room, where I rejoiced in having an elegant, but redundant, fireplace lined with William de Morgan tiles. The setting was sufficiently bucolic for one of my colleagues to be able to smoke his pipe out of the window, between classes. Other beaks gathered for a cigarette in the porch, since it usually took boys a little while to arrive from classes elsewhere on the Hill.

After he had been installed for a few terms Head Master Hoban reviewed the salaries being paid to various masters and I received a note from him saying that there appeared to be a discrepancy between the amount I was being paid and that of some colleagues. Fortunately, I was able to produce the letter that Dr James had sent me when I had queried the salary he had offered me on my appointment, on the basis that I was earning more at St Lawrence. Jimmy had characteristically replied that it would be "churlish to argue," agreeing to match the salary I was receiving at St Lawrence. So I replied with a copy of that letter, adding that I hoped the Head Master would agree that it would be "churlish to argue." I heard nothing back, but my salary was not reduced. However, I imagine my reply did not endear me to its recipient!

One thing Michael Hoban didn't change at Harrow was comparatively light teaching timetables. Afternoon or evening school was only on Mondays, Wednesdays and Fridays and one usually had a free run on one of those afternoons. So, without the House commitment, one had quite a lot of free time. One term I volunteered to attend a course on behalf of the English Department at the Helen Arkell Dyslexia Centre at Parson's Green, which meant a weekly afternoon trip to the Fulham Road. The point of this was to understand more about the causes of dyslexia and its treatment. One learnt that it often afflicts very intelligent children, boys more often than girls. When fellow participants heard I was from Harrow School they asked enthusiastically if Harrow was contemplating a dyslexia unit. They were disappointed when I explained that I was attending so that we could distinguish more accurately between boys who were genuinely dyslexic and those whose parents were merely attempting to use it as a bogus excuse for lack of attainment.

At the behest of my friend the Chaplain, who ran the Naval Section of the CCF, I agreed to be his Second in Command. We had a lively and instructive time one Easter holidays when we took twelve boys up to the Clyde estuary to join a naval MSV - a Merchant shipping vessel. It had a civilian crew, who ran the engines and supervised our navigation. The boys were billeted below decks in one large cabin, with cooking facilities for our meals. I'm not sure how we survived the cuisine, but I do remember being put ashore most evenings so I could use a civilized latrine! And halfway through the week we took all the boys to the public bathhouse in Dunoon, or some such resort, so they and we could use the slipper baths! Regular Wednesday RN Section sessions at school were far less entertaining, however. A lot of time was spent on learning different knots, under the eagle eye of a visiting Petty Officer. I think we also did Aircraft Recognition. Field Days were more entertaining, as we visited various naval establishments and sometimes even got to sea for a while.

On Thursday afternoons for some time I used to travel up to the Italian Institute in Belgrave Square for an Italian conversation lesson. This led me to set up an annual Easter trip for senior boys to Florence and Venice, of which I have many happy memories. It was the time of the Red Brigades in Italy and, after encountering a demonstration in Florence with the Carabinieri firing tear gas canisters, which the boys joyfully collected as souvenirs, I decided to limit our trip to Venice in future years. In Venice we always stayed in the Pensione della Salute da Cici, conveniently situated in the Dorsoduro district, close to Baldassare Longhena's magnificent Madonna della Salute church. There are many tales of our adventures over the years in Venice, such as the time the boys cut down a Communist banner that was hanging from the nearby Accademia Bridge, or the time they nearly got into a fight with some of the tough Burano boys. Fortunately old Cici (it's short for 'Giovanni'), and his son Renato, were understanding hosts and the boys mostly behaved themselves well. One of the party went on to found the Pret a Manger sandwich chain and others sent me cards from their honeymoons in Venice. Yet another became the Art critic of the *Church Times*! And I'm still in touch with some of them and glad that I introduced them to the joys of Italy and Venice in particular.

Another task that I was pleased to take on to fill my afternoons in the summer was as Master in Charge of the school's open-air swimming pool, rather quaintly named Ducker. It was located over a footbridge across the Watford Road at the bottom of the Hill. Although I was nominally the master in charge, I wasn't required to supervise the sessions for general school swimming, since Mr Campkin, the resident Ducker Attendant, was responsible for that. His wife also sold snacks from their little bungalow by the poolside. My duties were solely concerned with coaching the swimming team, three afternoons a week for about 45 minutes, organizing matches and accompanying the team to away fixtures. I enjoyed having the pool to myself before the boys were admitted. It had originally been a lake and had been concreted while retaining its graceful curving shape, with a bridge over the centre. Before I took over it had been decided to heat half of the pool, by inserting a wooden barrier under the bridge. For matches, an elaborate contraption of floating lane dividers had to be anchored in the heated end. When inspectors from the local council came to check on safety arrangements they advised that it was necessary to have a team of six attendants, three on and three off duty, in order to supervise the huge curving pool, one of the biggest in the country. That, of course, was the beginning of the end for Ducker. Now the school has a smart new indoor pool and swimming takes place year-round. But I still have memories of walking back from the old Ducker across the fields, humming the song *Ducker*:

'When the afternoon is over
  And the evening brings the breeze,
  And the sunset glories hover
  Round the steeple and the trees,
  In the twilight as the shadows
  Come to meet us o'er the plain,
  We will wander through the meadows
  Up the Hill and home again.'

It's sung in waltz time! After the new inside pool opened and Ducker became redundant it was bought by some oriental religious sect, but I believe they were refused permission to build there and so for many years Ducker remained as a sad ghost of its past.

There was a charming custom that boys leaving the school would have a small pocket-sized photo taken to present to friends and masters they liked with their address and a leaving message. Some long-serving masters used to display these photos ranged around the picture rails of their reception rooms. Not having any picture rails I invested in two large albums sold for the purpose by the school photographers. I have around 300 of these photographs and they chart the changes in the ten years I was a Harrow master. In the early photos the boys are rather formally posed, often in their tails, taken by the school photographer. Over the years they become steadily less formal and more inventive, often taken by friends, sometimes with psychedelic drawings or sketches. Finally some of them, not content with a photograph alone, press into service logos from beer cans on which to paste their photos! I wonder whether the custom survives in this digital age.

After ten years it was time for me to move on to pastures new and, I hoped, eventually to be able to seek ordination in the Church of England. Dr James, as a parson's son, had warned me that the Church of England was changing its traditional role and wanted to present a more radical face. I had already attended one Selection Conference for the Ministry from Harrow, which had resulted in my not being recommended and it was clear that I needed to widen my teaching experience, preferably in a less traditional establishment. A former Harrow colleague of mine had moved on to become Head of Arts at Welbeck College, the Army Sixth Form College, and he suggested I first join him there for a term to widen my experience.

Alas, I didn't realize that I was setting sail for a rougher passage than I had anticipated

Chapter Six

Craignez Honte

Welbeck College

Welbeck, the Defence Sixth Form College, was an Independent School for boys planning to join the technical regiments of the British Army. They came from very different backgrounds from those I had previously encountered, so I was certainly able to widen my experience. The College had been set up in the early 1950s at Welbeck Abbey, the Duke of Portland's seat up in the Dukeries, a few miles from Worksop in Nottinghamshire. The 8th Duke had decamped to Kenya and the estate was administered by Lady Anne, daughter of the 7th Duke, who lived in a smaller house on the estate, at some distance from the Abbey. It was an odd coincidence to find that our nearest educational neighbour was Worksop College, the school that I had been interviewed for down in London, before I accepted a post at St Lawrence College in Ramsgate.

Welbeck Abbey was an extremely impressive home for the College, but the State rooms were not included in the lease, the College being confined to the basement and the upper storeys of the great house. Some time after my stay there it was decided that the school needed room for expansion and it moved away from Welbeck to purpose-built accommodation. Sadly, the Ministry of Defence has now decided to close the school, as an economy measure. This means that a route for cadets from a wider social background than formerly has been lost. It was heartening to see the boys' confidence building during their time at

Welbeck, irrespective of their previous academic experience.

Welbeck Abbey is extraordinary, in that much of it is underground! Down in the basement the walls of the pre-Reformation abbey are still visible. I was privileged to be given a tour of the Strong Room by the butler, with its huge collection of impressive silver. Among the interesting curiosities are the one-pearl drop-earrings seen in the portraits of Charles I, and worn by him on the morning of his execution; also the silver-gilt chalice from which he received communion on that fateful morning at Whitehall. The chalice bears the following inscription: "King Charles the First received the communion in this Boule on Tuesday the 30th of January, 1664, being the day in which he was murthered."

There is also an underground railway, which was used to get food from the kitchen to the lift up to the Dining Room. The underground passage was the main route for boys and staff from their living accommodation on the upper floors of the Abbey to the teaching rooms and gym, which were also underground, lighted by windows in the roof, known as 'bulls'-eyes.' The gym was actually the former picture gallery and ballroom and, as such, must have been unique in being underground! Its construction had cost enormous sums and involved the removal of vast amounts of solid clay by up to 1,500 workmen. There was still a fine selection of family portraits and other pictures ranged around the walls, but, sadly, some of them had suffered from the ravages of basketball games. Works by Sir Joshua Reynolds, de Mytens, Tintoretto, Snyders, Bassano, Breughel, Van Dyck, Holbein, Kneller and Lely were amongst those that caught my eye. This vast room is 158 feet long, 63 feet wide, and 22 feet high.

This extraordinary set-up dates back to the 5th Duke of Portland, William John Cavendish-Scott-Bentinck (1800-1879). He was a recluse, known as "The Invisible Prince." He liked to take men unawares, popping up from various underground tunnels on his estate. He was a cynic who shunned his fellow-men, yet some of his employees saw him as a kind and considerate master. There have been various reasons put forth to account for his withdrawal from the society of his peers. It was said that he was smitten with leprosy, that he had an incurable skin disease; then that his love affairs had gone awry when he was a young man, with the result that he became a woman-hater, then a hater of mankind generally. One tunnel stretched towards Worksop and it was said that the Duke would drive to the station via this tunnel in order to take a train to London, where he would lead a relatively normal life. Another passage led to the old riding school, built by the Duke of Newcastle in 1623, but since converted to other uses, such as a library and a church, after the erection of a new riding school. Beneath it are great wine cellars with subterranean communications.

Tunnel entrance at Welbeck Abbey.

One of the Duke's descendants, Timothy Bentinck, now the 12th Earl of Portland, is also well known as David Archer in the long-running BBC radio serial. He was my Captain of Swimming at Harrow. The dukedom died out when the 9th Duke died in 1990.

I was accommodated in Lord Henry's suite on the ground floor of the great house. It had a splendid bathroom, with a throne-like w.c, which was flushed by pulling up a lever to one side of the mahogany seat which opened a flap in the bottom of the lavatory basin. Unfortunately the woodwork which surrounded it was attractive to cockroaches, so Rentokil had to visit regularly. There was also a huge and equally splendid antique bath, with enormous brass faucets.
Splendid as my surroundings were at Welbeck, I found it was a very lonely life. I had no contact with the two boarding houses on the upper floors and my friend Frank lived in Worksop town. He had left Harrow to become Headmaster of Truro Cathedral School, but the demands of keeping a failing school going had taken a toll on his health, with his voice now reduced to a croak. He was the kindest and most civilized of men and had been an Attorney in his native Scotland before joining the staff at Harrow. From Welbeck he retired back to Edinburgh.

It was three miles or so down the drive before one left the Welbeck estate. At night I could hear the plaintive baaing of the hundreds of newly shorn sheep in the surrounding fields. As the summer term went on I had the formal gardens closer to the Abbey to myself. The famous literary hostess Lady Ottoline Morrell had lived in the great house after her half-brother William succeeded to the Dukedom of Portland in 1879. She recorded that she also felt very isolated amongst all the splendour of Welbeck. Eventually she escaped, to become an external student at Somerville College, Oxford and married the Liberal MP Philip Morrell. They set up house at Peppard, near Henley-on-Thames, before moving to nearby Garsington Manor. Her patronage was influential in artistic and intellectual circles, where she befriended writers including Aldous Huxley, Siegfried Sassoon, T. S. Eliot and D. H. Lawrence, and artists including Mark Gertler, Dora Carrington and Gilbert Spencer.

I took my meals at Welbeck in splendid isolation, in a small dining room off the main dining hall where the cadets in their army pullovers ate in their two house groups. The nearest cinema was over twenty miles away in Sheffield. On the way one passed the Sitwells' family home, Renishaw Hall, sitting rather grimly above the coal mines from which the family's wealth had come. Worksop town itself had little to offer in the way of entertainment. My main memory is of a very large number of travel shops!

My teaching timetable at the College was light. The aim of the Arts Department was to broaden the cultural background of the boys who had concentrated on science and maths at school, since they were bound for technical regiments. So I was able to meander among some of the byways of English Literature, as well as covering major authors like Shakespeare and Dickens. My predecessor in the post had helpfully left me his notes on such topics as, 'Who really wrote Shakespeare's plays?' so I was able to get the class interested in Sir Francis Bacon, for example, by adopting this approach. There were absolutely no discipline problems, of course, since they were all on their best behaviour as they hoped to go on to Sandhurst! I confess that this sometimes made for rather somnolent lessons and I missed the cut and thrust of normal school life.

By a lucky coincidence, two of my oldest friends, Digby and Judith Anderson, had moved from Buckinghamshire up to Heanor in Derbyshire, within what passed for easy reach up in the Dukeries. Digby had a post at Nottingham University. Heanor was a mining town and its main claim to fame is that D. H. Lawrence had grown up in Eastwood, just three miles away. The Andersons are tremendous cooks and being able to escape from my depressing solitary meals and evenings at the College for their convivial company made an enormous difference to me. I can still hear Gounod's Saint Cecilia Mass blaring out as we played a recording cheer our spirits after dinner!

It was not easy to move from Welbeck back to an ordinary school. I was offered a post at Shebbear College, a Methodist boys' boarding school in beautiful North Devon, which would have been just as remote as Welbeck and reluctantly decided I should have to accept it. At the eleventh hour the Headmaster of Welbeck called me to say he had been contacted by the Headmaster of a school that would suit me much better, but he couldn't tell me which it was until I withdrew from the post at Shebbear, because of Headmasters' rules about poaching staff! This put me well and truly on the spot, but I decided I must trust his advice and duly withdrew from Shebbear. I was then informed by the Welbeck Headmaster that David Raeburn, the Headmaster of Whitgift School, Croydon, would like me to accept a post at his school for the coming September, for which I had been interviewed some time earlier. He had already appointed one master, but now found he had a second vacancy and would like me to have it!

Chapter Seven

Vincit Qui Patitur

Whitgift School

Whitgift School is a large independent day school for boys in South Croydon, which was founded by John Whitgift, Archbishop of Canterbury, at the end of the sixteenth century. It had originally stood in the centre of Croydon, along with the almshouses of the Foundation. In 1931 the school moved to Haling Park, in South Croydon and the Governors had the foresight to retain their freehold lands in the centre of Croydon. In the 1960s they developed the Whitgift Centre, a complex of shops and offices. Consequently it's now one of the most generously endowed independent schools in the country. This enables them to offer a large number of free or assisted places to boys of high academic ability, thereby keeping the school full and academic standards high.

The English Department was a thriving one, with four other male colleagues, under the benevolent oversight of Dick Glynne-Jones, the Head of Department. It was good to get back to teaching a broad spread of year groups, except the youngest. (They joined at 10 years of age!) For the GCSE exam we had our own arrangements with the Board. The boys had to submit their own anthologies, made up of poems they liked, and explain why they had chosen them. This involved much more work than simply teaching to an external examination, but it was also more satisfying. I recollect feeling very much in need of a chocolate boost after some particularly demanding lessons, which necessitated a quick trip down the drive to the confectioner's on the Brighton Road during a free period.

Most mornings at Whitgift still began in the traditional way with an assembly for the whole school in the impressive school hall. As at my own school, Latymer Upper, it was usually taken by the Headmaster, although there was also an Anglican clergyman on the staff, who celebrated a termly Communion service. The boys were well behaved at Assembly, with prefects, in impressive purple gowns, keeping an eye on them as they assembled and dispersed.

David Raeburn, the Headmaster, was a bundle of energy, bustling forth from his office at the centre of the building. He was particularly keen on drama, and often produced plays himself - so there were echoes of my own old Headmaster at Latymer. He had a number of theatrical friends, Ned Sherrin of the famous ground-breaking television satirical programme *That Was the Week That Was* being prominent amongst them. I think he hoped I would put on plays as well, but I had other plans. Being at a day school within easy reach of Blackfriars by train meant that I could join the Southwark Ordination Course which involved attendance for two evenings a week at lectures given by distinguished theologians at a church near that station. We were also expected to write a number of essays each term and sit an annual examination at London University.

Another attraction of the Whitgift job was that the school provided subsidized accommodation, although rents increased each year until the fifth year, by which time one was expected to have found one's own accommodation. Since I was still paying a mortgage and other charges on the house I shared with my widowed mother in Oxford that was not a practical option for me. But I hoped that, after completing the three year Southwark Course, I would be ordained in the Church of England's ministry and able to apply for a School Chaplain's post.

The flat the school provided turned out to be on the second floor of a shabby Victorian house in a road that backed on to the school estate, so I could make my way through a wooded patch behind the house to school each morning. Not only was Croydon a depressing place to live - the flat was even worse! Access was by a bare grimy communal staircase that no-one ever seemed to clean. Being on the top floor, I didn't feel inclined to tackle the whole filthy staircase, so I just had to learn to ignore it. It was more difficult to ignore the stink from the drain inspection chamber just outside the front door however, when it was blocked up! I never saw the other occupants of the flats, which were shared with Trinity School, also part of the Whitgift Foundation. There was no form of heating in my attic flat, except electric power points. I bought an oil-filled electric radiator, which took the chill off the sitting room, and a fan heater with a very long lead and a timer switch. This I set to wake up to some warm air in the freezing bedroom. I would then carry the heater with me into the bathroom to provide some warmth for my ablutions. Finally, I would carry it into the kitchen so I could eat breakfast in some comfort.

Unsurprisingly, I couldn't wait each Friday to start the gruelling two and a half hour drive to Oxford, arriving home in time for supper. Driving back to Croydon on Sunday evenings was equally taxing, with the prospect of the grim flat to look forward to.

During the summer terms I used to escape after school on the occasional fine day down the Brighton Road to that elegant resort, where I had friends. One of my former St Lawrence boys had a flat in an elegant Regency terrace above the sea front and it made a refreshing change to breathe the bracing sea air of 'Doctor Brighton' and get away from Croydon. I also had a former pupil at Sussex University, who had been a regular member of my Venice parties from Harrow. Alex and I used to meet up for a meal before I drove back to Croydon.

On one occasion, after a particularly convivial evening which involved going on to a club after dinner and drinking Singapore Gin Slings for some reason I cannot recall, I was warned by Alex as I prepared to drive back to Croydon, "Do be careful- one of your rear lights isn't working!" There was nothing I could do about it at that time of night but to drive as carefully as possible back along the Brighton Road until I reached the motorway section. I was well aware that Brighton is exceptionally well provided with Police officers to cope with the summer crowds. Sure enough, shortly before the motorway, I became aware of the flashing lights of a police car on my tail, carefully as I had been driving. "Are you aware that one of your rear lights isn't working, Sir?" came the expected question, to which I explained that it had only been pointed out to me earlier that evening, so I had no time in which to get it fixed. Then came the question which I had been dreading; "Have you been drinking, Sir?" Of course I had to admit I had and next came the request to take a breathalyser test. An electric device was produced into which I was to breathe. I prayed hard and gingerly breathed a gentle sigh into the officer's machine. As I did so I recalled that I had read that, with the old test, if the crystals turned green it meant you were over the limit. To my horror a green light appeared on the machine. I stammered out, "What does that mean?" I'm afraid the policeman may have thought I was taking the mickey. Anyway, he was clearly displeased with the result, which I put down to a miracle to this day! I was allowed to go on my way, having been warned to go carefully with my defective rear light and get it fixed as soon as possible, which I duly did, not wishing to have any more encounters with the Law!

Sandwiches and coffee were available at the lectures in Southwark on Tuesdays and Thursdays, but no alcohol! Not that it would have mattered, as I took the train to Blackfriars very conveniently from South Croydon station, just near the school. Then, on Friday evenings, I would speed off as soon as possible on the horrendous drive via the South Circular Road and the A40 to my mother's house in Oxford, arriving in time for a late supper. She always provided something for me to take back on Sunday evening to eat on Monday evening, which only left Wednesday to be catered for by myself.

All went well with the lectures and I enjoyed meeting the other participants and the lecturers. The first year was devoted to the Old Testament and I duly passed the end of year examination. Next year it was the turn of the New Testament and again the exam was not a problem. The Revd Professor Leslie Houlden, formerly Chaplain of Trinity College, Oxford and then Principal of Cuddesdon Theological College, was our distinguished lecturer and Tutor. However, to be accepted as an official candidate for ordination it was also necessary to be recommended by a Selection Conference organized by ACCM - the Advisory Council for the Church's Ministry. I duly went off to the Conference at Almondsbury, outside Bristol, with high hopes that this time all would be well, after having not been recommended some years before as a candidate from Harrow.

Unfortunately my confidence proved to be misplaced. The Selectors were concerned that I didn't seem to have a stable parish background, since I had got a friend who was a vicar in the Southwark diocese to sponsor me from his parish in Lewisham. My real parish church was St Mary Magdalen in Oxford, a well-known Anglo-Catholic stronghold where I had worshipped since I was an undergraduate. I was told the Selectors were unable to recommend me for ordination. This left me in a quandary. I couldn't face staying in my school accommodation for three more years, nor could I afford another mortgage to buy my own flat. It was also unthinkable to suggest to my mother that she move down to Croydon, away from the roots she had put down in Oxford after my father's early death in 1971.

Whitgift School

Fortunately David Raeburn, the Headmaster of Whitgift, came to my rescue again. There was an English post going at Dean Close School in Cheltenham. David knew the school well, since he had used its open-air theatre for a series of his Greek drama productions, the culmination of a holiday course he ran in the school's accommodation. If I got that post I hoped to transfer to the Oxford Ordination Course. I would have the backing of the Oxford parish of St Thomas the Martyr, where an old university friend had just been appointed vicar and would be glad of my help, with three churches to look after in his benefice.

Chapter Eight

Verbum Dei Lucerna

Dean Close School, Cheltenham

I hastened to apply to Christopher Bacon, the Headmaster of Dean Close School, for his English post and was delighted to be called for interview at the school in Cheltenham. Fortunately, I was forewarned by his very helpful Secretary that I would be expected to teach a demonstration lesson - something I had never had to face before or since, although I gather it is now commonly required. I had no idea what to prepare, but an old friend who was Head of English in another school came to my rescue by supplying me with the ideas for a lesson which had stood him in good stead. This involved reading poem LXIII from A. E. Housman's *A Shropshire Lad* to the class. Housman had said that the poem came easily to him, except for one verse, over which he had struggled. The point of the lesson was to get the class to discuss which verse they thought that might be. And, since we don't know the answer, it provides plenty of scope for discussion. Perhaps readers might like to look the poem up and form their own view? The beauty of this lesson was that it could be adapted fairly easily to any age group from 13 to 18!

So, armed with a supply of photo copies of Housman's poem *I hoed and trenched and weeded,* which I would just happen to have with me, I drove off to Dean Close. I was conscious that it was a strongly Evangelical school, but the reader may recall that my first permanent teaching post had been in a similar school, at St Lawrence. Indeed, the two schools were rivals in many ways, not only academically, but as hockey-playing schools. So I knew the culture, and I was also able truthfully to say how much I had enjoyed my four years at St Lawrence. Like St Lawrence, Dean Close had become co-educational, so this was only my second experience of teaching girls, as well as boys. I found it a very good mix and my trial lesson went down well with the Fifth Form, even with the Headmaster crouching on the floor at the back of the Portakabin which served as the classroom!

A couple of days later I received a call from Christopher Bacon, the Headmaster, offering me the post of English teacher and resident House Tutor of Tower House. He asked me if I would undertake to support Chapel and also attend the weekly Common Room prayer meetings in the Chaplain's rooms, which of course I was happy to do. These occasions were interesting, in that they always began with an 'exchange of news,' which was a sort of sanitized gossip session. One often learnt a great deal about one's colleagues by keeping quiet and listening! Such as the young master whose car had been parked outside the young Assistant Sister's flat all night! He left soon afterwards, I'm afraid - but he and Sister have been happily married since, and for many years! So perhaps our prayers worked!

An enormous sense of relief swept over me as I shivered in my flat in Croydon on that chilly February evening taking the Headmaster of Dean Close's call. The Summer Term at Whitgift flew by and, towards the end of term, I duly passed the London University New Testament examination and made arrangements to join the Oxford Non-Stipendiary Ministry Course in the Autumn.

Dean Close School sits a little way out of the centre of Cheltenham, on the Lansdowne Road in the largest private land area in the town. First, one passes a number of large Victorian houses, which form the core of the Pre-Prep and Preparatory Schools. Then comes Shelburne, one of the Senior Girls' Houses, next to the Headmaster's House and other school buildings. The magnificent Headmaster's House, with its galleried hall, was acquired during the headship of the Revd Douglas Graham, a larger than life character with a Boxing Blue from Trinity College Dublin. Douglas Graham's chaplains did not have an easy ride. Should the Chaplain be just a minute late coming in to take Chapel, Douglas Graham would produce his watch and then begin the service from his own stall!

Dean Close School

The school was originally named the Dean Close Memorial School, in memory of Francis Close, Vicar of Cheltenham for over thirty years and then Dean of Carlisle. He had founded Cheltenham College for boys, the Ladies' College and the Teacher Training Colleges that are now part of the University of Gloucestershire. But he didn't found Dean Close School! He was a very firm Evangelical and his sermons during the Cheltenham Festival race meeting, when he complained of the town becoming full of "Pimps, Prostitutes and Papists," were legendary. He also railed against drama, preventing the reconstruction of Cheltenham's theatre after it was destroyed by fire in 1839; against the oratorios of the nearby Three Choirs' Festival which represented a 'perversion of God's house'; and against the evils of tobacco (see later!). So, when it seemed his educational foundations were not remaining true to their Founder's principles, a group of local Evangelicals decided to set up a school that *would* remain true to them!

Girls first joined the school at the end of the Sixties, initially as day pupils only, around the same time as at St Lawrence College, that other Evangelical Public school stronghold, where I taught from 1965 to 1969. So I felt at home in such an environment. At that time the girls were still in a minority, as far as numbers went, but their accommodation was superior to the boys' in those early days. Because there was more competition for girls' places in those days, long before most other boys' schools had bowed the knee to co-education, the girls tended to be rather brighter than the boys. Or was it just that they worked harder? In any case the result was that in the two Sixth Form English sets in each year the top set had just one boy in it, and the reverse was true in the lower set! I felt rather sorry for the boys, but it didn't seem to worry them in the least!

In order to maintain decorum the Headmaster enforced the "Six Inch Rule," which meant that pupils should never be closer to each other than six inches. It wouldn't have been sufficient in Covid times, but it did serve to remind the boys to respect the girls. Reading the horrendous stories in the press and on television in 2021 about the abuse met by girls in so many co-educational former boys' schools one feels that Dean Close managed the potential hazards extremely well. No doubt its distinctly Christian atmosphere helped in this. I gathered that Christopher Bacon, the Headmaster, had been a Baptist lay preacher. When the time came for his daughters' confirmation he insisted on the Chaplain administering believers' baptism to them, immersing them in the school's swimming pool! The poor Chaplain had to borrow waders and weighted robes from a Baptist minister!

The main Senior School buildings are along Shelburne Road – a red brick mass, with a slightly Oriental-looking tower. This was not actually part of Tower House, although I suppose it inspired the House's name. There were three other boys' houses at the time, as well as a day house and three girls' houses. My accommodation was at the opposite end of Tower House from the housemaster's flat and consisted of a large bedsitter with its own bathroom and lobby. It had previously housed the Second Master, who had also been previously Housemaster of Tower. I was reminded that I had inherited the Second Master's accommodation back at St Lawrence! On the other side from the boys' accommodation, the flat linked to the Science laboratories and classrooms, but my own classroom was in the large Portakabin, which at that time housed the three English Department classrooms. It was situated on the 'Railway Triangle' - land which had been reclaimed from a former branch line, which the far-sighted

Headmaster had bagged for school use. During lessons one could sometimes watch a procession of lorries dumping material on the site to level it up.

The building was not very soundproof and I was always conscious that my Head of Department, Peter Cairns, taught in the room which adjoined mine. Fortunately, Peter was the most tolerant colleague and it turned out that he was a friend of my Vicar in Oxford and a Choir Director and High Churchman to boot! The third member of the English Department was a pleasant, decidedly Evangelical young man, in keeping with the school's tradition.

The School Bursar at the time I joined was an old boy of the rival Cheltenham College, which considered itself a cut above Dean Close. He informed me that Dean Close School had no financial reserves and that I should regard plans for a new Dining Hall and a Theatre as pipe dreams! Both were badly needed since meals were still being served separately in two of the overcrowded former house dining rooms. A self-service system had been introduced, but it could barely cope with the numbers. In a praiseworthy effort to inculcate good manners and conversation a third dining room, which operated with family service, had been introduced, to which houses were invited by rotation in order to lunch with the Headmaster. It was a typical Bacon initiative to encourage civilized behaviour. And eventually he got his fine new Dining Hall and the old Bursar had to creep away to retirement! A splendid new theatre followed, after my time, and it was rightly named the Bacon theatre, after a great Headmaster who did not spare himself in turning the school around and raising standards.

The Chapel was another red brick building, with good proportions, but suitably plain inside to match the school's Evangelical character. However it was much tidied up and improved during my time at the school in the early Eighties by the Venerable Chandos Morgan, the School Chaplain, who had previously been Chaplain and Archdeacon of the Royal Navy. He completed the paneling around the East End of the Chapel and installed some attractive stained glass, acquired from a redundant church, in the cloister, He was the most charming and urbane of clergymen, but there was an essential steeliness under the surface, as one would expect from his previous post. He was extremely supportive of my ordination hopes, but also loved to tease me about my High Church tendencies: "Have you got your Sanctuary slippers?" was a favourite enquiry. He retired from school chaplaincy to a living in the City of London and I was delighted when he suggested I join him in taking the marriage service of one of my Old Harrovians (the one who had played the Pope!) who worked in the City. Of course, it had to be the Stock Exchange's parish church!

Another very ebullient clergyman on the staff of Dean Close as a housemaster was the Revd David Gibson. He was a great admirer of C. S. Lewis, to whom he bore an uncanny resemblance. He cajoled me into attending the school's thriving Christian Union, which met on Friday evenings in the Chaplain's Vestry-Classroom, with his office just off it. "Come and show the flag!" was Gibbo's hearty invitation and I didn't regret hearing his call to arms. A packed room of some fifty boys and girls attending voluntarily and singing rousing choruses was a tonic and a complete contrast to my Tuesday evening trips to Anglo Catholic St Stephen's House, the theological college in Oxford where my Ordination Course was based, and where we sang our evening office in the austere surroundings of the Cowley Fathers' former chapel.

Christopher Bacon was really my first example of the new breed of Headmaster. He was extremely 'hands on' in his running of his school and this thoroughness was exhibited in my letter of appointment. All the promises I had made at interview were carefully tabulated and I was required to sign a copy of the letter and send it back to him, so there could be no backsliding. I was happy with this, except for one item - I was, as at St Lawrence, required to take a commission in the school's Combined Cadet Force. Since I had been an officer in the Naval Section of the Harrow School CCF, I was expected to take on the Naval Section at Dean Close. Certainly this was preferable to the Army section, but it did involve doing a course at the naval base in Portsmouth. One was put up in the Officers' accommodation there and given temporary membership of the Ward Room. It was rather like an old-fashioned grand hotel! Unfortunately the training, for which I had no aptitude at all, was not such a picnic. It was also very boring and came at a time in the holidays when I was also marking examination scripts from overseas for the Cambridge Local Examination Board. I remember sitting up late at night ploughing through the scripts, which left me prone to falling asleep during the lectures in the day!

There was no arguing with Christopher Bacon, because he would persist, claiming, "You know I'm right!" It was tempting to compare his attitude to that of the infallibility of the Pope, but that would not, of course, have gone down at all well in such an Evangelical establishment! So I was saddled with the Naval Section every Wednesday afternoon. In my innocence, I had not expected compulsory CCF activities to include the girls, but, of course, it did. I could never get over the sight of the girls parading in battledress along with the boys. Of course, nowadays such sights are taken for granted, both in the armed forces and in the school corps.

The Naval Section was extremely popular with the Dean Close girls during my time. In fact we ended up with just one solitary boy in the section! He was a shy youth who had achieved fame amongst his contemporaries during the Headmaster's sex education talk to new pupils by fainting as a particularly graphic slide was shown! I had to act as my own Quartermaster, or whatever the naval equivalent was, in obtaining and issuing kit to the cadets. I indented for smart shoulder bags for all the girls, but they were rather puzzled as to their use. I told them to put a brick inside their bag, so that they could take a swing with their bag at any errant Jack Tars when we visited naval bases! Fortunately the need never arose during our visits to naval establishments on Field Days.

I was ordained Deacon at Michaelmas 1994 and priested the following year in Christ Church Cathedral, Oxford, after four happy years at Dean Close. Talking to boys as I carried out my evening duties around Tower House I was asked if I would be becoming a second Chaplain at Dean Close. Chandos had already moved on to London and we had a lively new Chaplain in the Revd Daniel Young. I explained gently to the boys that I would find it difficult to read and assent to the School's Evangelical principles, laid out in a long document to which the Chaplain had to signify his assent. Of course, as usual in schools, the Headmaster got to hear of this conversation, but my views had been well known to him since my appointment interview and he bore me no ill will. In fact, he made a point of driving over to Oxford to attend my First Mass in the very Anglo-

Catholic Church of St Thomas the Martyr and even came up afterwards to the altar rail in order to kiss my hands and receive a blessing. I was extremely touched. As so often, I had found that Catholics have much more in common with Evangelicals than either do with wishy-washy liberals!

After I was ordained deacon I insisted on being released from my commission in the CCF, on the grounds that it was an inappropriate position for a clergyman. Thankfully, our former Chaplain Chandos, who had been Chaplain of the Fleet prior to his post at Dean Close, had retired by then, and I got my way.

One extra-curricular activity that I did very much enjoy at Dean Close was play production. I was happy to be able to revive my Harrow production of Noel Coward's *Hay Fever*, but this time with REAL girls in the female roles. All went well until we reached the line, "Give me another of those DISGUSTING cigarettes!" Smoking was taken for granted in Coward's day, of course, but it was always going to be a problem in a school production, let alone one in a school named in honour of Dean Francis Close, who preached sermons against tobacco, as well as the theatre! I bearded the Headmaster, pointing out that smoking was integral to the text and, indeed, to the whole Twenties atmosphere of the play, but to no avail. As a biologist, Christopher Bacon had particularly strong reasons to oppose smoking on health grounds, as well as a matter of school discipline - to say nothing of the fire risks and the school's heritage. I recall that, back in the Sixties, just before the report came out that definitively proved the link between smoking and cancer, a number of schools had decided - or been about to decide - to permit sixth form boys to smoke in a common room or club set apart for that purpose, incredible as it seems today. Anyway, that was never contemplated at

Dean Close and neither would there be any smoking, however justified in the text, on the stage of the Flecker Hall! This building was the only venue the school could offer for drama at that time, unless one counted the open air theatre, which was a delightful venue for a summer play (and safer for smoking!), but impossible in winter. Flecker had been the first Headmaster of Dean Close for thirty eight years. Like many other headmasters, he had a difficult relationship with his son, the poet and novelist James Elroy Flecker, whose most famous work is *The Golden Journey to Samarkand.* I cannot imagine that he would have approved of the production of a play by Noel Coward in the hall named after him, let alone one that allowed pupils to smoke! So Christopher Bacon certainly had good reason for his opposition to my request! But what to do, without altering the whole laidback, slightly louche character of Coward's play? The answer came to me as I passed a party and joke shop in town: get a supply of 'joke' cigarettes! These were hollow stems filled with fine white powder. The actors had to remember to blow, rather than suck, the "cigarettes." As can be imagined this palaver produced great hilarity when the line, "Give me another of those DISGUSTING cigarettes," was uttered with a suitable grimace! I suppose these days the white powder might have led to suggestions that the cast might be snorting cocaine, but thankfully such thoughts were still far over the horizon.

I also produced Noel Coward's *Fallen Angels*, another period piece from the 1920s, with two marvellous parts for the right girls, although I had found excellent boys to play the parts at Harrow! The plot is basically about two wives whose husbands neglect them to play golf. They console themselves by drinking a lot and courting a glamorous Frenchman. At first sight, it doesn't seem a very suitable play for an Evangelical school, but it's all harmless fun and has some hilarious scenes, if played at the right speed. With the aid of the trick cigarettes again and plenty of cold tea masquerading as alcoholic drink, to say nothing of hired costumes originally worn by Fenella Fielding and Penelope Keith, it went off well and no offence was taken- except perhaps by the ghost of Francis Close!

Although he was a demanding and strict headmaster, Christopher Bacon was also a warmhearted and genuinely Christian man. His daughters were in the school and notably happy and normal, unlike some of the other Headmasters' children I've encountered. It was Christopher who broke the news to me of my mother's death in hospital in Oxford. She had a heart attack during the night in her 81st year, but managed to get herself into hospital in an ambulance. Unfortunately she didn't survive a second attack there. They found my contact address at Dean Close and rang the Headmaster who broke the news to me and, of course, gave me leave to go home and make arrangements. At least, as a deacon, I had been able to give my dear mother communion at the altar rail Sunday by Sunday in St Thomas', during her last few months.

One of the 'cases' Christopher Bacon took on to his staff (was I another, I now wonder?) was Iolo Davies, always known as Dai. Dai had been Headmaster of Cowbridge Grammar School, Glamorgan in his native South Wales. It had a history going back to the early seventeenth century, but the local education authority had turned it into a comprehensive school in 1973. That event, and a domestic tragedy which led to the break-up of his marriage, had turned Dai into an alcoholic. Christopher had determined to recue a fellow headmaster if he could, by taking him on to the staff as an additional Classics master. He was given a room at the other end from my flat, off the Tower House Senior dormitory. The boys' dormitories at Dean Close, like those in many other similar boarding schools in the 1980s, were divided into 'horse boxes': individual compartments with wooden partitions between them and a curtain across the entrance to give some privacy. Dai's room was double size and had its own door off the dormitory, and a private washbasin. For other sanitary arrangements he had to share with the boys. Fortunately, he got on very well with them - so well, in fact, that on occasions when he had had recourse to the bottle and was unable to get himself up the stairs to the dormitory, the boys would carry him upstairs to his room. I know that on one occasion at least he couldn't find the key to his room and simply turfed the boy in the bed opposite out of his bed, exclaiming, "Sorry old man, I need your bed!" Of course, I knew nothing of this at the time and I'm sure neither the Housemaster, who had a flat in another part of the building, nor the Headmaster, had any idea of the goings-on. More seriously, I was mortified when I met up with one of the boys after he had left the school early and he told me that he was regularly bullied in the house. I had no idea of this when I used to tour the house at 'Lights Out' most evenings.

At the age of forty-plus I was beginning to find the long days and evening duties in the House quite tiring, much as I enjoyed talking to the boys. My salary included my board and lodging, and breakfast and dinner were served to resident staff in the Common Room, while we lunched with the pupils in the self-service dining rooms. But Prep began in the House at 7pm, the same time as Dinner was served in Common Room. This was exactly the same arrangement as we had at St Lawrence College, back in the Sixties, but Christopher Bacon wanted House tutors to be physically present on duty in the boarding house during Prep. I had to point out that, since I had no cooking facilities in my flat, and Dinner was included in my pay package, I would be available in the Common Room during the early part of Prep, before moving to my flat in the House. There was also an attempt to keep me on site for the whole day when I was on House duty. So I was even rebuked for popping into town during a free period during school hours. I had never encountered these demands in my three preceding boarding schools and, in my mid-forties, I wasn't happy about such restrictions and demands.

Each morning at eight o'clock there would come a thunderous knocking on my door in the House. Two determined cleaning ladies would be waiting to come in to make my bed and clean the flat. So there was no chance of a lie-in or of missing breakfast! One of the benefits of this rather intrusive service was that my laundry was all taken care of by the ladies, being entered onto a list and checked off and mended by them where necessary. It's one of the features of life at Dean Close that I most miss! However, because of all these restrictions, I contemplated moving out of the House and even eventually bought a small one bedroom flat close to Cheltenham College, about a mile from Dean Close. I let it furnished until I might need it. One's salary was reduced if one lived more than a few miles from the School, but Bathville Mews was comfortably within the limit. It was also convenient for Cheltenham College's much more 'High Church' Chapel where I enjoyed attending some of their weekday evening services, at the invitation of their chaplain. Naturally, I kept this quiet at Dean Close. In fact, I never had to move into the flat, managing to keep criticism at bay in my role as resident House Tutor of Tower House. I imagine these days one would have been faced with an unequivocal demand to bow the knee or move out, but Christopher was kinder than that. And at least I didn't have to be carried up to bed like Dai! There were also, however, some pointed remarks about masters driving off down the A40! I had to attend lectures every Tuesday evening at St Stephen's House in Oxford. At weekends I wanted to check my house in Oxford and I also needed to be seen at St Thomas the Martyr, my sponsoring parish. So it was all a bit of a balancing act and I remain grateful to Christopher Bacon for his restraint in allowing me to complete my Ordination course.

After what was judged to be a suitable period I was duly sent off by Canon Wilfrid Browning, the Director of Ordinands for Oxford Diocese, to my third Selection Conference with the Advisory Council for the Church's Ministry. This time I was lucky. One of the selectors was a doughty Anglo-Catholic lady, a friend of my old friend Canon Roy Porter from my Oxford days. Together she and Roy fought a rearguard action in the General Synod against the march of Liberalism. When it came to my interview with her she exclaimed that it was ridiculous that I had been kept hanging around for so long. I knew that the Selectors had to reach unanimity on the suitability of candidates before they left, after the Conference, and I imagined she would fight her corner for me until the others gave in. Whether that was what happened or not I don't know, but I was recommended for ordination this time, at my third and final attempt!

When the time came for me to leave Dean Close, at the end of the Autumn Term 1985, following my ordination as an Anglican priest in Christ Church Cathedral and appointment as Assistant Chaplain at Highgate School, Christopher Bacon and his wife Jill invited me to a farewell dinner in their house. I'm ashamed to admit that, in the flurry of my last week at the school, this engagement completely slipped my mind. I had almost finished dinner in the Common Room when a call came through from Christopher: 'We're waiting for you to come to dinner, Richard!" I was appalled and rushed off as fast as I could down Lansdowne Road to the Headmaster's house. I managed to eat enough of my second dinner to do credit to the Bacons' generous hospitality and afterwards I thought the least I could do was to offer to help with the clearing and washing up. "Let me atone for my sins, by helping with the washing-up," I offered, blithely overlooking the theological faux pas I was committing, in suggesting to a strong Evangelical that Works could atone for Sins! Christopher wasn't going to let me get away with that! "Impossible!" he cried. I *think* he was only jesting!

Highgate School Chapel

Chapter Nine

Altiora in Votis

Highgate School

After I had been ordained as an Anglican Deacon at Michaelmas 1984, I began to apply for posts as an Assistant School Chaplain. But the problem, as I soon realized, was that I was now 43 years old and Headmasters tended to prefer younger men as Assistant Chaplains (if they had one at all) who would command a lower salary and might be good at sports into the bargain! I had thought it would be sensible to learn the job of Chaplain by starting as an Assistant, but it appeared my age would make that difficult. I applied to Wellington College for such a post and was astonished to find that the Master intended to appoint a priest on a three year contract only. So one would have been a second class citizen there, as I pointed out to him indignantly. I then remembered Highgate School had advertised for an Assistant Chaplain some weeks earlier and wrote to ask if I was too late to apply. "You are by no means too late," came the encouraging reply, with an invitation to meet the Headmaster, Roy Giles, and the Chaplain, Father Peter Stone, at the school.

I had known Highgate School from the outside since I was a small boy, staying with my grandmother in her house just off Southwood Lane, which runs up from the Archway Road to Highgate Village. The school dominates the Village, with its impressive-looking Chapel on the corner of Southwood Lane, opposite the Gatehouse pub. But it proved not to be so impressive from the inside. I was first conducted to the Chapel by the Chaplain, who was awaiting my arrival at the school gates. He was very welcoming and we soon established that we were on the same level of churchmanship: high! Moreover, so was the Headmaster. However, I couldn't help noticing the deplorable state of a row of boys' lockers along the corridor which led to the Chapel Vestry. Several had been kicked in and others had graffiti. I had seen enough schools to know what such signs indicated, but I wanted a Chaplain's post and put such thoughts deliberately out of my mind. The History classrooms along the corridor to the Chapel Vestry were partly subterranean and most unpleasant to teach in. In an attempt to improve the ventilation they had been fitted with a rather ineffective form of air conditioning. I was to learn later, when I had to teach in one such room, that most colleagues preferred to leave the air con. off, because of the noise it made. The main blocks of classrooms, including the Chaplain's, had windows looking on to busy North Hill, which meant that opening them led to heavy traffic noise. The main school buildings stood on what had effectively become a cramped one-way traffic island, although this has now been mitigated with a new traffic scheme.

My interview with Roy Giles went well. We established that we had much in common in our outlook as well as churchmanship. Roy even revealed that his first teaching post, before he moved to Eton College, had been at Dean Close School! As he put it, "I know exactly from what you are trying to escape!" Mindful of Christopher Bacon's kindness to me, in spite of our different religious traditions, I replied that there was also much I was grateful for at Dean Close. Apart from the fact that it was true, it is never wise to run down your present school or Headmaster at an interview for another job!

Shortly after my visit to Highgate, I was duly offered the post of Assistant Chaplain and accepted it gratefully, with only a few misgivings. As so often in the past, accommodation had been promised, but I had been given no specific details. However, I had formed favourable impressions of both the Headmaster and the Chaplain on my visit to the school and felt we shared religious and political outlooks. With hindsight. the first mistake after my appointment was that the Chaplain and Headmaster decided it would be best if I delayed taking up my post until I had been ordained priest at Michaelmas 1985. That meant staying on at Dean Close until December 1985 and then joining Highgate in January, 1986. I would then be formally licensed as Assistant Chaplain by the Bishop of Fulham, on behalf of the Bishop of London, during Evensong in Chapel.

My predecessor in the Highgate post was a layman who had left at the end of the Summer Term. So there was a gap in the Religious Education Department for the Autumn Term. The gap was filled by two young Anglo-Catholic clergymen who moved in Peter Stone's circles in the Edmonton area of the Diocese of London, presided over by the Anglo-Catholic Bishop of Edmonton. When I took up my post I discovered gradually that the previous term had been a disaster, since the very streetwise North London boys had run rings (almost literally) around the two young priests, who were quite frank to me about their inability to control their classes, when we met later at clergy gatherings. Their warnings came too late for me. As yet another clergyman, I was already set up for a lively welcome from the same boys!

Being completely inexperienced as an RE teacher, I hoped for some guidance from the Chaplain, but his mantra was,

"Chalk and Talk, Father." There were no textbooks, apart from the Bibles which the boys were supposed to have! I quickly managed to buy some useful course books for the Old Testament, which I studied with the younger boys, but there was nothing for the difficult year following, before nearly all the boys gave up the subject on choosing their 'O' Level choices. In an attempt to tame the unruly Remove year, the classes had been split in half for their weekly Religious Studies lesson, some time before my arrival. Even this failed to tame them, and, with no syllabus or resources, one was a sitting duck. On the other hand, I had a free hand in what I decided to do with them. I didn't have my own classroom, which was another problem, so I decided to book the school's video room at the top of the Science building for as many lessons with the Remove as possible. At least it was well out of the way of the Chaplain and most other colleagues and I had a completely free hand in choosing what to show them. Anything with a vaguely religious angle was grist to my mill.

I recall on one occasion I was showing the boys Lindsay Anderson's anti-Public School film *If*, based on his experiences as a boy at Cheltenham College, when in walked Theodore Mallinson, the retired master who ran the school's Old Boys' society, with a couple he was showing round. No comment was made by the imperturbable Theodore, our most faithful supporter in Chapel! If challenged on my showing of *If*, I would have replied that it featured a Chaplain whom the Headmaster kept in a large drawer in his study! And what was the final scene at the end of the film where the rebellious boys mow down the Speech Day audience with machine guns all about? (I remember being told by the Head Master of Harrow that David Ashcroft, the then Headmaster of Cheltenham, had been shown a completely different script by Lindsay Anderson, the Director, when he asked for permission to film in his old school!) At least the film held the boys' attention and kept them quiet. Perhaps it even made some of them think as well.

When I wasn't 'teaching' up in the Video room, I was usually allocated a free classroom around the central hall or nearby. I soon discovered that there were boys running loose around the building during some lessons. Towards the end of term they would leave their classes to go through their reports with their housemasters during lesson time. Some of these boys developed the charming habit of attempting to kick open the door of the classroom in which I was teaching. Perhaps they were venting their feelings after receiving a bad report! Fortunately the doors were good solid Victorian ones, with locks for which I had been issued with a pass key, so I simply locked myself in with the class when such interruptions threatened! It was very satisfying to hear the thud of the boot of a frustrated kicker outside as he limped away nursing jarred limbs!

I had been looking forward to teaching 'O' Level and 'A' level Religious Studies, but there were no boys opting for the subject most years. The Chaplain had one pupil for 'A' Level when I arrived, but I was not offered a share of this. After four years we did have one boy who opted to do 'O' Level Religious Studies and Peter Stone told me I would be responsible for his tuition. The boy was not very bright, but I discovered his father was a Governor! No wonder he had been dumped on me!

The Chaplain informed me that we would meet each morning in Chapel to recite Morning Prayer, before the boys arrived for their weekly service. Each year group attended just once a week, because of the limitations of space in the Chapel. It also made it easier to control difficult boys, of course, and hopefully to target one's address at specific age groups. Housemasters and the Headmaster attended daily, Monday to Friday. On Sundays there was a Communion Service at 11am, often attended only by the Headmaster and Theodore Mallinson, with perhaps one other colleague. In the evening, Houses were invited on a rota once a term or so. Afterwards there would be a pleasant gathering with refreshments and a chance to meet parents. There were still three boarding houses when I joined the staff, but the writing was already on the wall for their survival. It was said that they were only kept going by the Headmaster's offering boarding places to boys who had scored badly in the Common Entrance Examination and would otherwise have failed to gain entry. Consequently, the other boys called them 'the thick boarders!'

Roy Giles, as Headmaster, did his best to maintain the civilized traditions of a boarding Public School. He and his wife did a good deal of entertaining in their house and always gave a dinner party when we had a visiting preacher at Evensong. Roy liked the Anglo-Catholic clergy, and had a wicked sense of humour! Christina, his elegant German wife, attempted to follow the same conventions that she had encountered during their time together at Eton College. So, when she judged it time for the ladies to retire to the drawing room, she would discreetly rattle her handbag. Unfortunately, to her consternation, I heard this often fell on deaf ears in North London!

Only once in my six years at Highgate was I asked to prepare a boy for confirmation. He was connected to the then Lord Ravensdale, a son of Sir Oswald Mosley, the former leader of the British Union of Fascists, and the boy was a boarder in School House. This was where I had ended up being accommodated myself, together with two other bachelors, on the top floor of the 'private' side of the house. I had a large bedroom, with a washbasin in it, and a small study opposite. The flat's communal kitchen was an appalling tip of unwashed cooking dishes and so on and the bathroom, which had the only loo in the flat, was also pretty gruesome. After a few years (!) I was able to arrange for a cleaner from the housemaster's quarters below on the ground and first floors to clean for us for some extra money. It was my own fault that I had ended up in this unpleasant accommodation, since Roy Giles had kept his promise at my interview by offering me my own flat in one of the other houses in Bishopswood Road. However, faced with the maintenance and upkeep of my mother's house in Oxford, after her death in the preceding November, and the sale of my small investment flat in Cheltenham, I did not feel up to taking on another flat which required redecoration and attention. So I had jumped at the offer of alternative accommodation in School House without having seen it. Once a term the fire alarms in the boys' side of the house would go off for practice and a procession of boys in their night attire would come through the door at the end of our flat that led to the boys' side of the house. Only once in my time at Highgate were the Chaplain and I invited to meet the boarders on their side of the house, but the Chaplain, never having worked in a boarding school, was so coy, and the boys reacted so badly, that we were never invited again!

I installed a silent refrigerator and a microwave oven in my bedroom and managed to get by with that for warming up ready meals. It was possible for resident masters to eat in the School Dining Hall in the evenings, after the boys, but it was a grim business with only two or three diners on most evenings. As at Dean Close and Whitgift I zoomed off home to Oxford most weekends, and very much resented the Chaplain's insistence that I should drive back early every other Sunday morning, in order to take my turn to celebrate Holy Communion for himself, the Headmaster and Theodore! This insistence meant, of course, that I could not be available to take any services in our three churches in Oxford on those Sundays. We also celebrated Holy Communion during the week at Highgate on Saints' days and other occasions.

The Chaplain had his own flat further down Bishopswood Road, as did a number of other masters. Every evening he could be seen walking his two West Highland terriers up and down the road. I hoped that, as at Harrow, when accommodation became vacant one would be able to put in a bid for something better than my shared flat in School House. The Headmaster's house was also in the road, and, later, another one was found for the new Deputy Headmaster. There were also three boarding houses in Bishopswood Road: School House, where I lived in the attic, had originally also been the Headmaster's residence, as at Harrow. It had been built just after the retirement of the formidable Victorian Headmaster, Dr Dyne, to accommodate a large number of boys in spartan conditions, in great contrast to the comforts of the private side. Dyne was a great flogger and it is recorded that he had beaten the poet Gerard Manley Hopkins, when he was a boy at Highgate. Interestingly, two other poets were connected with Highgate: T.S. Eliot had been a master in the Junior School and John Betjeman had been one of his pupils there, before moving on to Marlborough College.

Eventually a desirable small house close to the school up in Highgate Village became available for masters' accommodation and I hoped my request to move there would meet a favourable response from the new Headmaster, Richard Kennedy. I was soon disabused of any such hope, as it was allocated to a young incoming bachelor Assistant Director of Music. This, of course, was a straw in the wind to indicate my standing in the new Headmaster's eyes.

Once a year there would be a service in St Michael's Parish Church in Highgate Village to commemorate the School's Founder, Sir Roger Cholmeley, a former Lord Chief Justice and local landowner, who decided to found a charitable school "for the good education and instruction of boys and young men" in Highgate and the local parishes. On 27 April 1565 he was granted by Edmund Grindal, the Bishop of London, some land on the site of the old gatehouse to the Bishop's Park and Hermit's Chapel (opposite the Gatehouse pub, which still exists). There was a school song about Sir Roger, with a rousing chorus about 'Sir Roger Cholmeley-o" which had traditionally been sung on this occasion, until, according to the Chaplain, the boys started stamping their feet in time to the lusty chorus and it was dropped from the service.

From time to time there would be a Confirmation service in the School Chapel. I can only recall one during my six years at Highgate and that caused a logistical problem. In common with many other Public School Headmasters, Roy Giles considered himself to be the Ordinary of the Chapel. This meant he always entered the Chapel last and then the service could begin. However, when the Bishop of Fulham came to administer confirmation *he* naturally expected to enter the Chapel last! Fortunately there were two entrances to the Chapel, so they could enter simultaneously at their separate entrances. Thus Peace was preserved and Honour satisfied! There were also two organs in the Chapel: the original instrument, housed above the vestry, and another in a gallery at the West End. This had Tracker Action, I was informed. It had been acquired from a redundant church in Marylebone at the instigation, I understood, of Roy Giles. Poor old Arthur Wallace, the long-suffering Organist and Assistant Director of Music, had to run round the outside of the chapel to play this second instrument as required. At least it was better for him than the notorious occasion when boys had persuaded him by some ruse to get on to the ledge outside the second storey window of the Music School in Dyne House and then closed the window against him!

Peter Stone insisted that I should follow his lead in always wearing clerical dress, not only in Chapel and classrooms, but on any social occasions in school circles to which one might be invited. I had a pocket for my pen inserted into the top of my cassock so that I could upstage him by wearing *full* clerical dress, but the first time I appeared in it I got so many catcalls from the obstreperous Highgate boys that I reserved my cassock for Chapel use only from then on! However, because of the circumstances of my departure, I decided not to wear my clerical collar at a leaving party for the Chaplains. I was greeted with a stare by Peter when he saw this, but I countered by showing I was wearing a white plastic wristwatch strap. "It's all right, Father. I've got it round my wrist," I announced. He was not amused.

Although no sportsman himself, Roy Giles had been assiduous in fronting a successful Appeal that produced a magnificent new swimming pool and gymnasium. In spite of the Chaplain's opinion that gymnasia were insidious pagan institutions, he and I were both delighted to be able to use the new pool before morning Chapel on some days. The building was named after Highgate's longest-serving master, Theodore Mallinson, to mark his outstanding contribution to the school. In his eighties he would still walk from Highgate to the West End of London and his club, the Athenaeum. Theodore still ran the school's Old Boys' society, coming into school every morning in term, as well as being prominent in the Old Cholmeleian Masonic Lodge. I suppose it was inevitable that the new building should soon be christened by the boys 'Mally Pally,' a reference to nearby Alexandra Palace, popularly known as Ally Pally.

One of the things that Peter Stone and Roy Giles were most pleased about in the Chapel was the introduction of an aumbry, in which the Blessed Sacrament was reserved. A great deal of trouble was taken to get a design that fitted perfectly into the Victorian Chapel and the Bishop of London, the Right Reverend and Right Honourable Graham Leonard, came to install the Blessed Sacrament. He had known the school from the time when he had been Archdeacon of Hampstead. I had been to see him during his time as Bishop of Willesden to enquire about ordination while I was teaching at Harrow. When he came to Highgate he made a point of enquiring of me about my school accommodation. He wanted to know exactly where it was, but, anxious not to cause a fuss, I told him it was ok.

After the Bishop's visit, conscious of the susceptibilities of the majority of our congregations, I was instructed by the Chaplain *not* to acknowledge the Real Presence of the Lord in His Sacrament by genuflecting as we passed the aumbry on our way in and out of Chapel. I was deeply unhappy about this pusillanimous instruction, which I ignored if I was by myself. Needless to say, I found the aumbry empty and neglected when I returned to Highgate for a memorial service a few years ago.

The day-boy Houses at Highgate loosely followed geographical boundaries. This meant that some houses drew on the old Highgate families and produced very pleasant civilized boys. Some of the more outlying areas produced some very rough diamonds. There were quite a number of Greek or Cypriot boys, from the Tottenham area, but they mostly had good manners that belied their rough appearance. I rather enjoyed having my priestly hands kissed by their devout mothers after Sunday evening Chapel! The Headmaster (who had been an Eton beak) used to raise his hands in horror as we passed some of the scruffiest boys, but he didn't rebuke them. It was noticeable, too, that he avoided addressing the school as a body. While we still had a 'family service' sit-down lunch in the Dining Hall it was possible for him to give out a brief notice after lunch. Grace was still said, but all that changed when self-service was introduced under the new Headmaster, Richard Kennedy, in September 1989. He began by taking the bull by the horns and addressing the School, assembled in Big School, but he employed the Senior Master to stand on stage until there was silence and he could then walk on with dignity.

The reader may not be surprised to hear that my early years at Highgate were not happy ones. After two miserable years I even applied unsuccessfully for the same Chaplain's post at Magdalen College School in Oxford that I was to be offered eventually some six years later! I was told by my colleague, the Chaplain, at the time that it was far too soon for me to attempt to move to a full Chaplaincy. Since they had experienced difficulty in finding applicants for my post they clearly didn't want to have to go through the process all over again. But later, when I had become more or less reconciled to my lot at Highgate School and had got the boys under control, I found I was suddenly being encouraged to apply for posts at other schools under the new regime.

The appointment of a new Headmaster in 1989 had come as a shock to the Chaplain and myself. Roy Giles was still well under sixty, but it seems the new Chairman of Governors wanted a new broom. The Chairman was a ruthless accountant and at his final Speech Day Roy Giles didn't miss the opportunity to introduce into his speech the words, "Accountants, who know the price of everything and the value of nothing." I was seated immediately behind the Chairman and watched the back of his neck turn scarlet. The Chaplain insisted I dress as he did for these occasions: cassock, Oxford M.A. gown and hood with preaching bands and carrying our mortarboards. Roy always began his speech with, "My lords, ladies, Reverend Fathers and gentlemen," or similar words, which I imagine did not greatly commend us to the North London audience.

I found two very good ways of getting to know the boys outside the realms of Chapel and RE lessons. Firstly, I persuaded the then Head of English, Cyril Hartley, to let me have some 'A' Level English teaching, which I was very much missing. Wily old Cyril agreed, provided I also took a lowly fourth form for him last period on Friday afternoons! He was a motorcycle enthusiast and liked to change into his leathers in the masters' cloakroom and roar off before the last lesson.

Secondly, I revived my Easter parties to Venice. They had been a great feature of my Harrow years. The first party was in Roy's last year as Headmaster and it went off well, without any problems. I took around fifteen sixth-formers single-handed, staying in my old favourite Pensione Alla Salute da Cici. The next year, with Richard Kennedy as Headmaster, was more difficult. He was appalled that I had led the previous party single-handedly and insisted on my taking another master as an assistant. Fortunately an old school friend of mine, who had been a master at Bloxham School, was also known to the Head, since he had done his teaching practice there for the Oxford PGCE course. So it was agreed that my friend would come as my assistant. Unfortunately he was not familiar with the ways of the Highgate boys and his sharp rebukes led to their pushing an offensive note addressed to him under the door of his room in the Pensione. I had to work hard to calm both sides and stop his threat to send the boys' rude note to the Head. By then the boys and I had got to know each other and the pleasant time we enjoyed naturally helped with relations back at school when Term began, along with the fact that I had gained much more respect as an 'A' Level English teacher than as a mere Assistant Chaplain! They could also actually see I was a human being and was not sewn into my clerical garb!

One of Richard Kennedy's new appointments was to bring in a Deputy Headmaster from outside, instead of following the former custom of appointing a Second Master from amongst the most senior masters as his right hand man. I think this is one of the most significant changes the Public schools have seen in my time. It means that, instead of a traditionally-minded master who might well defend staff he feels have been unfairly treated by a new Headmaster, most schools now have a Deputy Headmaster who has come from outside and owes his position, and depends for his advancement, entirely on the Headmaster. My memory of Barnaby Lenon, the new Deputy Head, at that time is of a keen young master, who – like Roy Giles - had come from being a beak at Eton, where, I believe, he had been Head of Geography. He used to carry a clipboard around with him, which I found slightly intimidating. Barnaby Lenon moved on in due course to become Headmaster of Trinity School, Croydon, the sister school of Whitgift, where Andrew Halls was his Deputy before moving to Magdalen College School to take over as Master. And Barnaby Lenon finally became Head Master of Harrow. So it has been very much what a dear old female parishioner of ours used to call, "Cat's cradle!" I ran into Barnaby and his wife looking round St Thomas the Martyr parish in Oxford, where I worked as a Non-Stipendiary priest, after my retirement. I was hosting a party in the Jam Factory, now a restaurant and bar, which adjoins the church, so I was able to invite them both in for a drink for old times' sake. On another occasion, at a party at the North Oxford Conservative Association I found Barnaby in charge of the Bar! I couldn't resist remarking that it seemed unwise to put a former Head Master in charge of the drinks. On reflection, I wondered if this innocent remark might have appeared to carry more undertones than I had intended!

Returning to Highgate School, another of Richard Kennedy's appointments, although technically in the gift of the Chairman, was that of John Rae, former Headmaster of Westminster School, to the Governing Body. Kennedy had been Rae's Head of Mathematics at Westminster. It was amusing to see the notice he put on the Common Room board about this, since masters had been used to seeing, on the same board, articles from *The Times* by the same John Rae with emendations and scathing comments added by Roy Giles! Roy couldn't stand Rae's grandstanding as an educational pundit. I gathered many of the Westminster boys had felt the same about him. Rae had also been my predecessor but one as Master in Charge of Swimming at Harrow, but I hardly expected this to weigh in my favour with him as a Governor. His wife Daphne had, in fact, published a book which had been highly critical of Harrow. It circulated amongst colleagues on the Hill in a brown paper cover.

Early in his third year as Headmaster, Richard Kennedy announced that the Chaplain would be retiring. Since the main purpose of my appointment seemed to me to be to assist a High Church Chaplain who was getting tired, it was obvious that my position would now become precarious, unless, as I had come to hope, I were to succeed Fr Stone as Chaplain. I was soon disabused of any such hopes by Kennedy, who informed me quite bluntly that he would not be appointing me as Chaplain and that my post of Assistant Chaplain would cease to exist. Peter Stone had accepted early retirement with generous compensation, but no such offer was made to me. It became obvious that part of Kennedy's remit was to get rid of Roy Giles' two Anglo-Catholic Chaplains. We had apparently done a good job of getting up the noses of the North London parents and some of the Governors!

My 50th birthday fell at the beginning of what was to be my last year at Highgate and I was determined to celebrate it in some style. I had arranged with the Bursar to have the use of Big School, and with the Caterers to take care of food and drink for some hundred guests. Prior to the party I celebrated a birthday Mass in the Chapel. I felt obliged to invite the Headmaster to the reception, in spite of his threat of redundancy. He looked very ill at ease standing in a corner of the Hall and I'm afraid guests in the know rather cold-shouldered him. I should have made more of an effort to introduce him to my guests, but many of them were already aware of my situation and I didn't want to risk any barbed exchanges. When the question of my paying for the use of Big School arose, the Bursar, who was a very decent man and knew of my impending redundancy, told me he proposed to forget it!

Reluctantly, I had started applying for Chaplaincies at other schools, but 51 wasn't an ideal age for a candidate! Girls' schools, it was true, sometimes preferred an older man, for obvious reasons, but I had no experience of teaching in a girls' school. Eventually, however, I secured an interview at St Catherine's School, Bramley, near Guildford and was offered the post of Chaplain. I had met the outgoing Chaplain previously, when we had both been candidates for a Chaplain's post at one of the Woodard boys' schools. He had got the job and persuaded me to come down to Bramley and take a look at St Catherine's. The school chapel was a small but charming Tractarian building. There had obviously been a High Church tradition in the past, but now there was a separate Head of Religious Studies who was a Fundamentalist Evangelical. This seemed to me to be a recipe for trouble! Apart from the Headmaster and the Chaplain, I only met one other man on the teaching staff and remained uncertain as to whether I should accept a post there, should one be offered. It *was* duly offered and immediately, with indecent haste, Richard Kennedy posted a notice in the Masters' Common Room announcing my appointment. I saw him and told him I had grave doubts about the job and was going to withdraw my candidacy. To be frank, I saw no reason to give him an easy way of getting rid of me to a job I didn't want. In fact, I told him I would contact my union, the Assistant Masters' and Mistresses' Association (AMMA), with a view to obtaining legal advice. He replied smoothly that, of course, I had a right to consult them, so I made it clear that I intended to fight his proposal to make me redundant and bring in a new younger Chaplain. I had actually been teaching a heavier timetable than the Chaplain and taking an equal part in Chapel, so I felt particularly strongly about it.

I arranged a meeting at AMMA's headquarters with their genial Secretary who dealt with Independent School members. He advised me that it was essential that I should actually apply for the post of Chaplain when it was advertised, in spite of already having been told by Kennedy that he would not appoint me. I followed these instructions with a full application to Kennedy, together with names of referees. I had hoped to include an old college friend who had become editor of *The Times* as one of them, but unfortunately he declined on the reasonable grounds that he knew nothing of my work as a school chaplain. I still wonder what effect the implied threat of including the Editor of *The Times* as a referee might have had on Kennedy and his Governors! Needless to say, I was not appointed, or even interviewed, for the Chaplain's post, which went to an outside candidate who was Chaplain of a small girls' school in Sussex.

Eventually a hearing with the Highgate Governors was arranged for me, along with my Representative from AMMA. I went down to meet him on the morning of the hearing in his office behind Trafalgar Square and, rather to my surprise, he took me to a slap-up lunch across the river in the Festival Hall. "Might as well have something back from all your subscriptions," was his cheerful remark as we tucked in. This was hardly my priority as a preparation for the forthcoming meeting with the Governors! When we reached the school, we were ushered into the presence of the Board of Governors, only a few of whom I had met, ranged around a long table opposite me. My Representative, to my disappointment, had little to say at the meeting. Fortunately, I had made some preparations. So, when the Headmaster announced that, leaving aside my Chaplaincy work, my contribution to 'A' Level English teaching wouldn't be missed, I was able to circulate copies of a letter the new Head of English had sent me, apologizing for not having English classes to give me in the forthcoming year, but looking forward to finding some for me the year after. I had the pleasure of seeing the Headmaster flush and lose his composure in front of his Governors at this point! I later learnt that the Head of English had subsequently been berated by him for not forewarning him of the letter's existence! Nevertheless, we made no progress with the Governors, in spite of the attendance of the Bishop of Edmonton. One of the Governors actually suggested that it would be no problem for me as a clergyman to find a living somewhere. I explained that, having been ordained as a Non-Stipendiary Minister, it was incumbent on me to find my own employment in the secular world. The bishop remained silent, but looked uncomfortable.

It was clear to me that AMMA had no appetite for a fight. My Representative actually warned me that Highgate School was a wealthy institution to take on. Fortunately, my cousin, who is a solicitor with his own practice, had assured me I had a good case in law, since I had been undertaking more than half of the teaching and chapel services already. Nevertheless the Governors, of course, backed their Headmaster. When it came to the question of compensation for redundancy they stuck to the bare legal minimum that they were obliged to pay me, based on my six years at the school. I refused to settle for that, vowing that I would take them to a tribunal.

As the Summer term drew to a close I had almost resigned myself to leaving chaplaincy work and I got into the habit of scanning the job advertisements in the *Oxford Times* at home at weekends for anything that I might have a chance of picking up locally. I even contemplated a job as a College Porter, since I knew of another former school chaplain who had taken on just such a post on retirement from his chaplaincy at a girls' school near Oxford. Fortunately, I had just completed the mortgage payments on the house I had shared with my mother in Oxford, after my father's premature death, and I could also begin to draw a reduced teacher's pension on the basis of early retirement. So I could survive financially. Scanning the *Oxford Times,* I noticed a small advertisement for a part-time English teacher at Magdalen College School, Oxford. That would suit me perfectly, if I could get them to take on an old lag! And, to my relief, I could, and they did!

So, now that I had secured a post back in Oxford, I was even less disposed to let Highgate School off lightly. Eventually, under pressure from AMMA, the Governors increased their compensation offer, together with an early retirement package, which I accepted at the eleventh hour, at the end of August, thus avoiding both sides having to face a tribunal, with all the attendant publicity that might involve. I was conscious that, while the publicity a tribunal might bring could embarrass Highgate School, it might also not help me in my next post.

One of the most unexpected aspects of my six years at Highgate was that the school magazine *The Cholmeleian* carried no exituary notice about my contribution to the life of the school. After six years' service to the school I found this surprising. Of course, it could carry an unspoken implication that I had left under a cloud, which was completely untrue. However, now that the school is "under new management" I have been invited back for various events and have received a warm welcome from both Old Cholmeleians and former colleagues.

Chapter Ten

Sicut Lilium

Magdalen College School, Oxford

Having been up at St John's College from 1960 to 1963 and then having had my home base in Oxford since 1967, I was used to seeing the boys of MCS around the city and I was also prepared for the rather makeshift nature of some of the school's buildings, back in 1992.

The school was founded in 1480, primarily to provide choristers for Magdalen College chapel. In 1894 the College built an attractive boarding house for the School on the other side of Magdalen Bridge from the college buildings. But later, in 1926, the College statute referring to the School was altered. Whereas before it had ordained that the College 'should always maintain the School,' it now ran, 'So long as the grammar school of the College in Oxford is maintained....' So the school entered a long period when its survival seemed to be in doubt. As a result, temporary classrooms were built along Cowley Place, most of which are still standing today. It wasn't until the 1950s that new permanent buildings began to be erected, including the new Chapel-cum-Big School facing the roundabout at the Plain.

It was during Peter Tinniswood's Mastership, from 1991, with his business expertise (he had been Head of Business Studies as well as a Housemaster at Marlborough) that the school's finances and governance were really sorted out. In the past I understand the Fellows of Magdalen had tended to leave School matters as a late item on the agenda at their meetings. Peter worked to get an Independent Board of Governors established, with College representation, rather than dominance. A much longer lease was also negotiated with the college for the school's buildings and facilities, to encourage donors to fund new buildings.

When I presented myself for interview in Trinity Term 1991, I found the Master was still sharing a Portakabin as an office, together with his Secretary and the Bursar. I received a warm welcome and was soon introduced to the Head of English, a charming man just a few years older than me. I discovered that he and my former Head of Department at St Lawrence College, now the Headmaster there, were the Senior Examiners for the Oxford and Cambridge Board's 'A' Level English examination. They had recently been unjustly accused, according to a newspaper report I had read, of favouring independent schools in their marking! I was beginning to hope by then that I might fit in at MCS, even though it was only junior English that was on offer. The other member of the Department was a younger man whom the Head of English had tutored at Pembroke College, where he used to do a bit of 'moonlighting' from his job at MCS!

I was relieved to find there was no nonsense about teaching a demonstration lesson. I had not taught the 11 to 13 age group since my temporary posts at Frays College in 1960 and 1963! After a very friendly conversation with the Master it was all arranged for me to join MCS as a part-time teacher of junior English from Michaelmas Term 1992.

Coincidentally, I met the Chaplain in the pleasant Masters' Common Room, which was located in one of the 'temporary' buildings dating from the 1920s. One could walk straight into it through the Common Room garden from Cowley Place in those days. The building still stands, but the Common Room has been moved into one of the new buildings, and security has been installed all around the site: a sad sign of the state of our present society. Anxious to reassure the Chaplain that I would not be wishing to encroach in any way upon his territory, I told him I would not be wearing my clerical garb in school. I was somewhat nonplussed when he replied that he never wore his either!

In September 1992 I arrived at MCS to take up my new post. I was delighted to find it was still a very traditional Common Room, with a friendly old-style Second Master, who had been up at St Catherine's College with one of my old Oxford friends, who was an old boy ('Old Waynflete,' after the Founder William Waynflete) of the school and now a local Anglican parish priest. From my friend I had heard many entertaining stories of his time as a chorister and boarder at the school in the 1940s and 1950s. Looking around the Common Room, it seemed as if things had not changed very much since those times. There were many colleagues of my age or older and only a couple of full-time female teachers, one of whom was French and taught it. After a year or two, when I was established on the staff, Peter Tinniswood confided in me that it was "that lot" over in the Common Room that worried him. This was when moves were being made to introduce 'Appraisal' into schools, aptly described by one of my colleagues as, "that dishonest charade." The Common Room managed to keep it at bay while Peter was Master. I had assured him that his staff were mostly men with their own high standards - in fact, they reminded me of my own masters at Latymer. I don't think this reassured the Master as much as I had hoped it would. Anyway, his successor was quick to introduce the "dishonest charade!"

There had been one very important change, however, since my interview: boarding had greatly diminished and the substantial School House was to be utilized as a Junior department of the school the next year. Hitherto, with the exception of the youngest choristers who sang in the College Chapel, most boys had joined the school at eleven years of age. There was also a smaller entry at thirteen, mainly from prep schools, notably the Dragon School in North Oxford. They more than compensated for those choristers whose voices had broken and who had not reached the necessary academic standard to continue in the senior school. The former choristers' parents would also be faced with finding full fees once their sons left the college choir.

The new Junior Department was a great success, with fees that undercut local preparatory schools. This enabled the eleven-plus entry to become more selective in turn, and thus academic standards could be raised eventually throughout the school. It had previously been remarked to me by my Bishop that he thought Magdalen College School should be doing much better academically than it was. The end of boarding also meant that the Master and Bursar could abandon the dilapidated Portakabin and move with their assistants into much more impressive accommodation in School House. The Master and his elegant wife Catharina also moved into the former Housemaster's flat there, which became very stylish. I remember particularly the dining room with a white-painted floor. But the electricity remained dodgy for some time, before conditions gradually improved. Before he became Head of Business Studies at Marlborough College,

Peter Tinniswood had been at INSEAD, the International Business School at Fontainebleau, near Paris, and I learnt Catharina had worked as a model at Valentino. So she brought a great sense of style into School House. I gathered she still used to do some work for Valentino during the Season. Catharina put her experience to very good use at MCS after a few years, by organizing a Fashion Show, with girls borrowed from Oxford High School and Headington School and our own boys, wonderfully scrubbed up! It was the greatest fun, although some tongues were clicking at such frivolity!

On another occasion in Big School I produced Peter Luke's adaptation of *Hadrian VII*, a fantasy about a reforming English pope, based on Frederick Rolfe's novel of the same name. It was an adaptation of the production I had put on in Speech Room at Harrow nearly twenty years before and once again was a lot of fun. My Hadrian this time was the son of the Senior Censor at that time of Christ Church. If anything, the reforming English pope depicted in the play was even more relevant to developments in the Roman Catholic Church in the Nineties than it had been back in the Seventies.

Peter Tinniswood was a generous host, and not only at dinner parties. Should a problem occur that needed talking through, one would be invited upstairs in his house for a drink. He specialized in a delicious White Lady, a gin-based cocktail with Triple Sec and lemon juice added. And his and Catharina's two cats were called Gin and Tonic!

As I feared, as a part-time English teacher, I was to become a classroom wanderer and that didn't help one to get on top of the large classes of 11-13 year old boys. It was quite a tough time, especially as I was still licking my wounds after Highgate. As with all my Heads of English, one was given an almost free hand in what books one chose to use with the boys. I remember being taken aback when I was shown the English book room, which was not the tidiest of places, so foraging for sets of suitable books could be taxing. Oh for the simplicity of simply being able to order them from the School Bookshop and have them charged on the boys' accounts, as we did at Harrow!

Towards the end of my second year, the Master let it be known that he would be looking to replace my part-time post with a full-time English one, in view of the school's expansion, due to the success of the Junior Department. So I was encouraged to apply for Chaplaincies elsewhere. It had become clear to me by then that the current Chaplain was not happy in his post at MCS. I think he rather despised what he saw as 'Public School Religion.' Not only would he not wear his clerical collar, but he also declined to wear an academic hood on occasions such as the annual Commemoration Service in the University Church or the Carol Service in Magdalen College Chapel. Relations between the Master and the Chaplain had not been helped by the Chaplain's strong opposition to smoking in the Common Room. He led the moves to have it banned, as it eventually was, the few smokers (amongst whom the Master was prominent) being confined to a smaller windowless room. Indeed, the Chaplain's animosity towards the Master had reached such a pitch that he wouldn't sit in his stall facing the Master in Chapel! Not surprisingly, he was applying for posts elsewhere. This put me in a difficult position, since, should we both apply for the same post, I felt he would be in the stronger position, particularly as he was considerably younger than me and had been a full Chaplain for some five years or so. In fact, he had been appointed by the previous Master, in preference to me, when I had applied from Highgate! But Peter Tinniswood merely smiled and said, "Leave it to me!"

I was not entirely surprised, therefore, to hear, shortly after this, that the Chaplain had been appointed as Head of Theology at Sherborne School, down in Dorset. Peter Tinniswood then offered me the post of Chaplain - for one year! I pointed out that this would be very difficult for us both, since I would have to be applying for a permanent post elsewhere almost as soon as I took up the post at MCS. "All right," replied Peter, "How about two years initially?" I gratefully accepted this offer and set about moulding the Chaplaincy according to my fairly traditional outlook.

My first task was to plan the daily Chapel services for the whole school a term ahead. So, as I had learnt to do at Highgate, I produced a sheet which laid out the readings and hymns for the whole term. I found this a very satisfying, if complex, task each holiday. I established a weekly pattern of services for the six days, Monday-Saturday, each week. The sixteen Choristers were excused attendance, in compensation for their heavy schedule over the road in the College Chapel. The rest of the school was expected to attend chapel, unless written requests to be excused had come from parents. The number of these was always in single figures during my eight years as Chaplain. A notable one came from the well-known novelist father of a pleasant Sixth-former, who always made a point of giving me his contribution to the weekly collection for charity that we held during Saturday Chapel.

Sunday services had ceased when boarding stopped. Once a week, usually on Wednesday, I would give a short talk on a theme that we followed week by week through the term. On Saturday there was Hymn Practice, which, to my relief, the Director of Music took for me in a most efficient manner. On Thursdays I introduced a voluntary Eucharist, held at the same time, and as an alternative to, the full school service. The Master willingly agreed to take the Thursday school service for me. A few years later I found his successor had passed this task on to one of the senior masters. The former Chapel had been turned into the Library after the new Big School-cum-Chapel had been built back in the Fifties and it made a very suitable and much more intimate venue for the Eucharist. I was able to beg the portable altar we had used for weekday Eucharists at Highgate from the new Chaplain there, as well as the Paschal candlestick, for which they now apparently had no use. The altar, when folded, fitted neatly under the big desk at the East End of the Library under the stained glass window and it made a very dignified setting for the Eucharist, when set up each week by the boys. I was delighted that about a dozen boys of all ages regularly attended. A few of them were Roman Catholics, which pleased me. When they asked if it was in order for them to receive at the altar I used to refer them to their own priest, and that usually resulted in their no longer receiving the Sacrament. However, most of them continued to attend, and even, in some cases, to be altar boys . Two of those Catholic boys from my time are now priests and I've enjoyed staying in the Venerable English College in Rome when they were seminarians there, as well as attending their ordinations. Three of my former Harrow boys, to my knowledge, are Anglican priests, so that makes the score 2-3!

Once a term we held a Sung Eucharist in the School Chapel with the school choral society (as opposed to the Choristers) singing the service and leading the hymns. We tried to link it with some suitable festival, usually

Ascension Day, All Saints' Day and Ash Wednesday. I even succeeded in imposing ashes on the foreheads of the choir and congregation, including the Master! Later on, I went so far as to introduce incense on this occasion and bought a thurible for the purpose. I also managed to increase the candles on the altar from two to four when my organist told me he had found a candlestick behind the organ which matched the odd one in the vestry. I had wondered why there were apparently only three of the very nice baroque silver candlesticks that matched the altar crucifix. I suspect these dated from the chaplaincy of Father Crusha, my very High Church predecessor in the late Thirties, who, according to a visiting Old Waynflete priest, had got himself thrown into the River Cherwell for his extreme views and practices! (I kept quiet at that point!) Since he was Patron of the living of Oddington on Otmoor, Fr Crusha retired from schoolmastering to appoint himself to his own living! He was also a Guardian of the Anglican Shrine of Our Lady of Walsingham in Norfolk and I have noted his name inscribed upon his former stall in the shrine church there.

In my first Hilary Term as Chaplain I managed to convince the Master to allow me to have a reproduction of the Taize crucifix fixed up above the sanctuary in the School Chapel. He agreed to its going up for Lent, but I 'forgot' to have it taken down! I was pleased to see that it was still there when I last looked, nearly twenty years on!

My predecessor as Chaplain had often kept his whippet in the vestry while he was teaching. When I inherited the room and its stained carpet I tried to get the Bursar to replace it, but with no success. I also suggested we needed a safe in the vestry, at which the Bursar enquired, "To keep the wine in?" I explained that all the vestries I had come across were provided with a safe for the chalice and paten and any other church silver, but the Bursar very sensibly replied that the cost of a safe would be much more than the two rather worn silver plated chalices that the school possessed. However, I had more luck in ordering two new altar frontals – All Seasons and Lenten purple - and a new altar covering for the portable altar in the Library.

I took over a small GCSE Religious Studies set from my predecessor. He and his female assistant had been teaching a multifaith syllabus and the boys - not by any means the brightest sparks at MCS - were quite confused between Judaism, Islam and Christianity. I swiftly decided we would stick to Christianity in future exams and the results improved greatly. My assistant was most insistent that our copies of the Holy Koran should be kept on the top shelf in the bookstore, in keeping with Islamic rules, and there they remained, unused, after she had departed for ordination. Another lady used to visit to talk about sexual matters to the Fourth forms. She always had a very large handbag with her and I heard there was much lewd speculation amongst the boys as to what exactly it might contain.

Things had settled down nicely at MCS during my second year as Chaplain. Peter Tinniswood was appreciative and said he hoped I would apply for the permanent post when it was advertised. I thought about this carefully. I was now 55. I was fairly sure there would be several much younger applicants, if it should be advertised. I already had my own house in Oxford and my somewhat reduced teachers' pension, plus what I had been able to put into a private pension while at MCS. So I was secure financially. I was also the honorary assistant priest in the parishes of St Thomas the Martyr and St Frideswide, two Anglo-Catholic strongholds in West Oxford, so I had my ministry there as well. I decided to go for broke! "Well, I'm too old to play that game," I replied to Peter, "I shan't apply if it's advertised." Peter thought for a moment and then, to my enormous relief, replied, "Ok, you can have it anyway!" So there I was: confirmed in the post I had always wanted! The whirligig of Time had come right at the end!

Just before the end of Hilary Term it was traditional for the whole school to go on a fairly long run through Christ Church Meadow, along the river and back up along the Iffley Road to school. There had been a similar run over Hampstead Heath for all the boys at Highgate at the same time of year and I couldn't resist pointing out to Peter Tinniswood, while we were both watching the boys come panting past us, that Richard Kennedy ran with the boys! He had been Head Boy and a keen runner when both he and Peter were boys at Charterhouse School. Peter took a drag on his cigarette and the expression on his face said it all! I've often wondered whether he took me on at MCS partly because Kennedy, his old school contemporary, had pushed me out of Highgate!

I started entering a team of Magdalen boys for the Prayer Book Society's competition for schools, which involved their declaiming suitable pieces from the 1662 Book of Common Prayer. The regional final was held at St Edward's School in Oxford and I found, to my pleasant surprise, that Michael Hoban, the former Head Master of Harrow, was Chairman of the Judges. He greeted me warmly, inquiring which were my boys. This impressed the boys greatly, even more so when they were placed first! P.D. James, the crime novelist, was a great supporter of the Prayer Book Society and I believe she paid for the prize, which was a magnificently bound and printed copy of the Authorised

(King James) Version of the Bible. The boy who won it generously presented it to the school for use in Chapel. I was delighted to be able to put it on the Lectern in Chapel and put away the Good News Bible, which I had inherited.

After another couple of years Peter Tinniswood moved on to become Head Master of Lancing College. I had known for a while he was looking to move and one of my colleagues with a very good ear for the grapevine had wickedly kept the Common Room informed of his applications. I had noticed a huge advertisement taking up half a page of *The Times* for the Headship of Lancing, which prominently stated, "Business Expertise Required." I immediately thought of Peter when I read that. Lancing, it was generally known, had been in some financial trouble for a while. And Peter had sorted out the finances of Magdalen College School admirably. So I wasn't surprised when I got a telephone call one morning break in the Common Room Secretary's office from the Provost of the Woodard Corporation, the Bishop of Guildford. He asked me if I was alone and I replied that only the Secretary was with me. The bishop insisted I ask her to leave the room before he spoke further, and then asked if I knew about Peter's application to be Head Master of Lancing. I had to confess that I didn't, but said that I wasn't surprised. He was anxious to know about Peter's support for Chapel and I was able to tell him that it was unwavering. At that moment who should come into Common Room and wave at me cheerily through the glass door into the Secretary's office but Peter himself! I told him about the call after his appointment: it does no harm for Heads to know that they are not the only ones who make background telephone enquiries about applicants! Bearing in mind Peter's well known smoking habits, it was suggested by some wags that Lancing, with its firm Anglo-Catholic tradition, was ideal for him, since he would be able to smoke unnoticed amidst the clouds of incense in the Chapel! I had been instructed that no service was ever to last over an hour at Magdalen, not that I was tempted!

Magdalen College School- The White Bridges

One of the features of the grounds surrounding MCS is the white bridges over the River Cherwell and they are actually featured in the stained glass in the Chapel window, to symbolize the bridge between Town and Gown that the school represents in its intake, as well as its geographical situation between the university and East Oxford. The bridges were made of wood, which needed replacing, so we thought it would be nice to make it something of an occasion. We invited Colin Dexter, the 'Inspector Morse' novelist, whose son had been in the school, to open the bridges after I had blessed them and sprinkled them with holy water.

After Peter's departure for Lancing in 1998, I was faced with the third incoming headmaster of my career, when Andrew Halls was appointed as Master of MCS. By coincidence, he had followed me, also teaching in the English Department, at Whitgift School. His father had also taught at Harrow County Boys' Grammar School, where I had done my teaching practice! So we had some things in common. And David Raeburn, the Headmaster of Whitgift who had appointed us both, visited MCS soon after, as one of the Inspectors of the Classics Department.

I only had four years to go until I reached the school's retirement age of 60. So I felt fairly relaxed about the situation, although I was well aware that Heads generally like to pick and appoint their own choice of Chaplain. I trod carefully and found I could fend off any unhelpful suggestions for changes in Chapel by suggesting that the boys would laugh at them. There was a notable occasion, however, when the boys *did* laugh in Chapel. As I began the service a muffled voice came from underneath the altar. Fortunately I grasped where the sound was coming from pretty quickly, leapt under the altar and pulled out from behind the frontal the offending loudspeaker, now detached from its wire. I took this seriously, since it is all too easy for services to descend into farce if such events become commonplace. So I insisted on the offending senior boys, who were soon discovered, being suspended for a period. I think the Master was probably rather inclined to be more lenient, but I stressed the need to make a firm example of such miscreants.

On Remembrance Day there were no such problems. I have always been impressed, in all the schools in which I've served, by the seriousness with which the boys take this service. At MCS the names of those who had fallen in the two World Wars and subsequent conflicts were solemnly read out by the Heads of their respective Houses. I re-introduced the hymn 'I vow to thee my Country,' much to the approval of older colleagues, and decorated the altar with votive lights, poppies and a wreath. We kept the Two Minutes' Silence perfectly and ended with the Last Post, played by one of the boys.

I was extremely fortunate in my relations with the musicians at MCS, remembering the problems at St Lawrence College, for example. The Director of Music was an enormous support and help to someone like me with little musical ability. He never objected to my sometimes esoteric choice of hymns and was always there to play the organ unless a boy was playing. There again, I was extremely fortunate with boy organists. One of them now plays regularly at my old college, St John's, and another, a former Chorister, is on the music staff at Brighton College, but also plays on Sundays in the church of a priest friend of mine in London. The Assistant Director of Music used to produce a beautiful Carol Service for me each year in the College Chapel, as well as the Commemoration Service in the University Church. I always felt a complete fraud when parents congratulated me on these services and I tried to give credit where credit was due.

I found the annual Carol Service in the College Chapel involved a tremendous squeeze to get everyone in, but I was determined, if at all possible, to avoid a series of services, such as we had to endure at Highgate. I was also determined to make it clear that the occasion was a *service*, rather than a carol concert, as some were prone to call it. To that end, I resisted parental pressure for the names of individual lesson readers to be listed on the service sheet. I was also determined to make the altar in the College

Chapel visible and acknowledged, rather than completely blocked by seats placed in front of it, so that the focus became the choir stalls, rather than the altar. Accordingly, I had a path cleared through the serried ranks of chairs and a space saved behind the altar for me to come from the Chaplain's stall to give the Blessing at the conclusion of the service. It was also necessary to get those seated with their backs to the altar to turn and face it for the Blessing. I found a good lunch with plenty of wine usually put me in the voice and mood to bark out the command, "Please turn and face the altar for the Blessing!" And they did, looking a bit sheepish!

I would also have liked to properly acknowledge the Blessed Sacrament, reserved in an aumbry to the South side of the altar in the College Chapel. The extra seating completely concealed it. But, recalling the difficulties at Highgate School Chapel, I judged this to be a battle too difficult to win. It was the main reason that I never even considered trying to install the Sacrament in the School Chapel at MCS. Apart from anything else, the Chapel's use as a dual purpose hall-cum-chapel ruled that out. For plays, all the seats had to be turned to face the stage at the opposite end of the building from the Sanctuary. And, in the summer, it became an examination hall, and services moved to the Sports Hall.

One of my most difficult occasions came after the death of Princess Diana in Paris. Peter Tinniswood rang me early in the morning to warn me that I would be expected to say something in Chapel. I tried, in what I said, to make the point that Her Majesty the Queen's generation, like mine, had been taught that a "stiff upper lip" was the way to behave on such occasions, rather than the modern emotional approach. Her Majesty was being criticized for remaining at Balmoral with Diana's sons and not coming down to London immediately and making some emotional speech. Eventually Tony Blair, the Prime Minister, was able to persuade her to address the nation and her usual quiet dignity "speaking as a grandmother," in that memorable phrase, carried the day. I also announced that the Eucharist in the Library that week would be a Requiem for the Princess.

The new Master, Andrew Halls, was debating ending Saturday morning school, which I suppose was really a hangover from the boarding days. Some of the older denizens of the Common Room missed the chance to catch up there with the Saturday papers, safe from being dragooned into shopping by their wives, but generally the change was welcomed.

After a year the Master asked me if I could do with an Assistant in the RE Department. Of course I jumped at the chance. He was going to interview a young master who had, he said, been teaching the subject at St Alban's School. Well, the young man was duly appointed and I set about constructing a timetable for him. I thought it would be a good idea if he took over some of the junior Divinity work, as well as helping with a Philosophy option in the Sixth Form which the Master was keen to introduce. I was looking forward to the promised slightly easier timetable for my last two years or so, but then came a surprise, which I should have foreseen. The Master said that there would, of course, have to be a reduction in my salary, commensurate with the reduction in teaching time! I was somewhat taken aback at this, and the warning I had previously received that the new Master could be "ingenious in his interpretation of promises made" sprang to mind! I had rather walked into his trap! However, since

I was already drawing my pension based on my leaving salary from Highgate, a reduction in salary wasn't going to make a great deal of difference, as the Master had no doubt already worked out. To sweeten the pill he suggested I might like to take a whole day off each week: how about Saturdays? Mindful that I already expected he would soon abolish Saturday morning school, I said I would prefer Mondays off, and so it was agreed.

During the course of the next year I began to realize that the pleasant young master who had been "sold" to me as an RE teacher was, in fact, a teacher of Philosophy, a subject the Master clearly wanted to introduce into the Sixth Form curriculum! It emerged that he had never actually taught Religious Education to junior forms! Nevertheless, he uncomplainingly put up with the forms I had already dumped on him. I felt a bit sorry for him, as the boys who opted for Philosophy in the Sixth seemed to be mostly my old lags from the GCSE Religious Education set! It also meant that numbers opting for Religious Studies 'A' Level, rather than Philosophy, were sometimes uneconomic. Strangely, it worked out that I was able to run the subject every other year. One year, only one boy, whose parents were keen Roman Catholics, opted for the subject. Miraculously, we found that the 'A' Level Religious Studies classes at nearby Headington Girls' School would more or less fit into his timetable, so he was farmed out to them for the subject. After a month or so I became aware that he had taken to wearing eye make-up, but I decided it was best to turn a blind eye to it, since I was not actually teaching him. Presumably the teachers at Headington took such matters in their stride.

When it got to that stage towards the end of the summer term when timetables for the coming year are arranged I was surprised to find the Director of Studies had timetabled me for all five days of the week, Saturday morning school having been abolished, as I had anticipated. I told him about my agreement with the Master to have Mondays off in exchange for a reduction in salary and he looked very dubious. Clearly he hadn't been told about this. Eventually he came back to tell me that he had been able to keep Mondays clear for me, but said we'd better not let the Master know! I replied that, since the Master and I had an agreement, there was no problem attached to his knowing! Nevertheless, for my last year I was made to feel that I had to keep my free Mondays under my hat. I should have thought it would have been pretty obvious, since I wasn't available to take Chapel on Mondays, but there we are! And I was very glad I had refused the Master's original offer to take Saturdays off!

Andrew Halls' predecessor, Peter Tinniswood, had appointed a female School Counsellor to help with pastoral matters. I had heard tales of boys winding her up with outrageous stories, but I kept out of her sphere. I was, however, surprised when the Master let me know that he proposed to dispense with her services. These days such posts are seen as indispensable, but I certainly wasn't aware of any great gap when she left. The most difficult pastoral matter I had to deal with at MCS concerned a boy in the Fifth form whose father was under police investigation for allegedly taking pornographic films of children. The boy's sister was at Headington School and the Headmistress and I had to attend the court hearings. As far as I could understand the alleged pornographic films he had taken were innocent ones of children's parties. On another occasion I was informed by the new Usher (in effect, the Deputy Head) that a suspicious man was filming boys at the school's Open Day. I had to escort him off the premises, while he loudly protested his innocence. It was all deeply embarrassing and I'm still not sure of the truth of the allegations that were made.

I had a very enjoyable 'A' Level Religious Studies set for my last year, consisting of four bright boys, whom I was pleased to be able to hand on to my successor for their second year. I had changed examination boards to Edexcel, so that we could continue to study St John's Gospel for one half of the syllabus. I booked myself in for a briefing conference with the Edexcel exam board, as it was a new paper. The Chief Examiner was very helpful at the meeting and told us there were six topics and six questions. So, back at school, we concentrated on them. In due course a specimen paper arrived and I set the boys to practice the questions in it. I then took them through their answers, showing them how they could be improved. Imagine my surprised delight when the real exam paper arrived with almost the same questions! Unsurprisingly, the results were good, with one boy scoring the almost unheard of mark of 94%! He went on to read Theology at Peterhouse, Cambridge.

There was only one occasion when I had a slightly sticky interview with Andrew Halls. He sent for me to ask if I knew who had been driving the school minibus the previous day. Of course he knew I had been, since I was signed in on the booking list! I confirmed I was the driver and he then revealed that he had received a report from a member of the public that the school minibus had been seen being driven recklessly round the city with a crowd of boys shouting from the windows! I explained that another vehicle had been trying to cut me up on the inside and that the boys had merely been shouting a warning. I was dismissed with a quizzical smile. At least I hadn't jammed the bus against the roof of an underground car park as a colleague managed to do!

On another occasion, Andrew Halls tackled me by saying that he had heard I didn't think the improvement in academic results at the school was anything to do with him. I explained carefully that he had arrived at the right moment, and had indeed been the right man, but that his predecessor had prepared the way by doing the heavy spadework and getting the Junior entry up and going, so that it was possible to be more selective with later entrants. No more was said.

Some time after I had left the school I was approached by Andrew's successor as Master at a social occasion at the school, when he came up to me and said he'd heard I didn't approve of him! This followed my interview in the *Oxford Times* when I expressed my regret that Magdalen College School had decided to take girls into the Sixth Form, to the dismay of two of the four private girls' schools in Oxford, the High School and Headington School, with whom we had previously enjoyed excellent reciprocal relations. I assured him it was nothing personal and reminded him of his predecessor Andrew Halls' excellent article in *The Daily Telegraph*, in which Andrew had defended the importance of boys' schools. Unfortunately, purely because of financial considerations, such principles seem to have been abandoned in recent years by many former boys' schools, at the expense of their sister schools. And, at the time of writing, there's a whole website and much news space given over to tales of sexual misbehaviour, mostly by boys in coeducational schools! What a surprise! I note also that the schools with the longest experience of co-education, with equal numbers of boys and girls throughout the school and long-established sexual education programmes, like Dean Close and St Lawrence, seem mostly to have escaped such scandal.

When my time as Chaplain and Head of Religious Education at Magdalen College School was up, according to my contract which specified retirement at the end of the academic year in which my sixtieth birthday fell, I was flattered that the Master asked me if I would like to stay on to come in and take the morning services for the school for an honorarium, as he put it. I was tempted since, of course, I knew I would miss the boys and the rhythm of school life. But then I thought about it. After a year, there would be two years worth of boys whom I didn't know from teaching them in class. They would begin to wonder who that old man was, who came to take the services and probably bored the pants off them. And, of course, I then realized it would mean that the Master need not advertise for a clergyman as Head of Religious Studies! So I politely declined the tempting suggestion and helped draft an advertisement for a priest in Anglican Orders!

The advertisement for a Chaplain and Head of Religious Studies duly appeared and we awaited applications. Out of a good field, only one of the applicants had the initiative to get in touch with me and arrange an informal discussion before his official interview. I was very impressed by him when he came to tea at my house, and soon made up my mind that he would be a good candidate. His religious tradition was Evangelical and my experience at St Lawrence College and Dean Close had led me to respect such a background. The other short-listed candidate was more Catholic-minded, but also, I suspect, rather too liberal. The Master had decided both candidates were to be invited to take a morning Chapel, simultaneously, which meant the congregation would have to be split between the

Chapel and the Sports Hall. The Master proposed to drop in on both venues. I ran through what would be required with the young applicant and, when it came to the Prayers, I remember he volunteered that he could pray extemporarily. I told him firmly that the Master, with his English teaching background, liked the Cranmerian language of the Book of Common Prayer. I like to think that may have helped him to win the day, coupled with his easy manner addressing the boys. He informed them that, amongst other things, he had worked as a "beach model" in Australia and they seemed suitably impressed. Fortunately, perhaps, the Master was in the Sports Hall with the other congregation and candidate at that point!

So my candidate was duly appointed and served six very successful years before moving on to a Headship. I told the Master later that he had been the only candidate with the gumption to get in touch with me and arrange a meeting beforehand and Andrew seemed a bit peeved that I hadn't told him before. But I didn't want to do anything to queer his pitch, and, since I was not part of the selection process, I didn't feel I had acted improperly in responding to a request for information!

On May Morning 2002, for the first and last time, I climbed the college bell tower with the choristers and Informator Choristarum (Choirmaster) just before 6am for the annual singing of a hymn, the *Hymnus Eucharisticus*, from the top of Magdalen Tower, a tradition stretching back over 500 years. The choir traditionally also sings a madrigal, *Now Is the Month of Maying*, following prayers for the city led by the Dean of Divinity. It was a fine morning and a great privilege to be invited in my last year as Chaplain to be up there with the choir above the milling crowds below on Magdalen Bridge.

May Morning Magdalen College

And so ends this account of what I have been tempted to call, *The Ups and Downs of a Schoolmaster*. But, leaving aside its lack of originality, such a title would be far too simplistic. I never expected to become a schoolmaster. I never expected to teach in such a wonderfully varied collection of schools, ending up back in my home city. And I never expected to be ordained as an Anglican parson and finally to be received into the Roman Catholic Church. Deo Gra

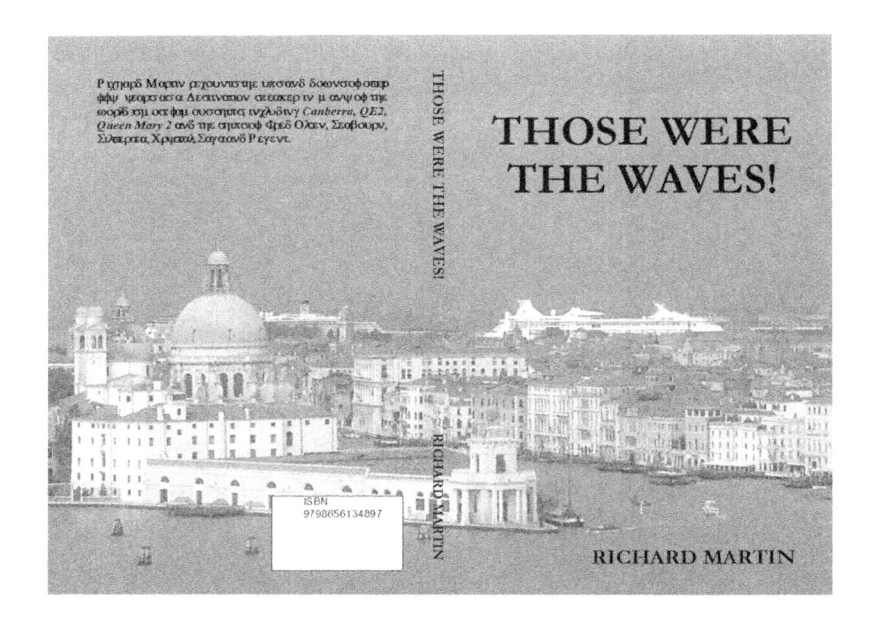

If you have enjoyed this book, you might also enjoy *Those Were the Waves,* Richard Martin's account of his other life, in vacations, as a cruise ship lecturer for over 50 years, on over 150 cruises, in ships ranging from the converted Channel ferries of the Chandris Line to the mighty Queen Mary 2 of the Cunard Line.

255 pages and over 40 full colour illustrations of ships and places.

Available through Amazon ISBN 9798656134897
or on Kindle.

Printed in Great Britain
by Amazon